# The Magimix Cake Book

# The Magimix Cake Book

## Tessa Hayward

First published 1985 by the Publishing Division of ICTC Ltd.,
632-652 London Road, Isleworth, Middlesex, TW13 4EZ

British Library Cataloguing in Publication Data
Hayward, Tessa
  Magimix cake cookery.
  1. Cake    2. Food processor cookery
  I. Title
  641.8′653      TX771

ISBN 0 907642 12 8

*I have had help and suggestions from many people but I would
particularly like to thank:*

  *Esmé Auer who, as well as producing ideas, did much of the cooking for
the photographic sessions. Lynn Hayes who has washed up more Magimix
Bowls than I would care to count.*

  *Pam Brierley who demonstrates the Magimix, who has been tester in
chief, and has fed back to me the comments of many of her customers who
have, although they may not have known it, also been trying and testing
the finished cakes.*

  *Edward Piper who has patiently and with great imagination taken all
the photographs and designed the book.*

  *And last, but not least, my husband and children who have eaten their
way through everything, including some very odd concoctions, and whose
only complaint seems to be that of expanding waistlines.*

Photoset by V & M Graphics Ltd, Aylesbury, Bucks
Printed in Spain by Printer Industria Grafica SA, Barcelona
D. L. B. 13868-1985

ICTC Stock Number: 54138

The dishes and china on pages 21, 25, 49, 71, 74, 81, 102 are from ICTC Ltd.

Home made cakes have a certain cachet to them and although they are perhaps not part of many people's everyday diet, they are frequently made in thousands of homes. No celebration, birthday, Christmas or whatever, is complete without a cake; few weekends with children or elderly relatives around are complete without a cake; no fête or bazaar is complete without a home made cake stall, in fact the list is endless, and the variety of different cakes that can be made is also endless.

I frequently meet people who tell me that a Magimix is more than a second pair of hands, but that it is disappointing as far as cake making is concerned. After further questioning I discover that they make their cakes as they always have; by the creaming method and process the complete mixture for far too long. Magimix cakes are exceedingly easy and quick to make and I always use the all-in-one method which I find works perfectly. However, before you start please read the recipe for Victoria Sponge on page 12, which explains the basics and rules to cake making in a Magimix.

The book contains what I hope is a comprehensive selection of cakes and I have tried to achieve a reasonable balance between the party 'flights of fancy' and the everyday cakes of the 'cut and come again' variety. I have devoted a chapter to the Magimix Whisk giving recipes for both meringues and whisked sponges, and another to choux pastry which is both easy and satisfying to make in the Magimix. The final chapter covers a wide range of cookies and sweet and savoury biscuits.

This book is intended to be practical and of real use to the Magimix owner: However I hope that it will also give you new ideas, new inspiration and new verve in the kitchen.

Tessa Hayward

All weights and measures are given in Imperial followed by the Metric equivalent. Use one or the other, but as the conversions are not exact do not mix them.

The eggs used throughout the book are size 2.

All spoonfuls refer to level rather than heaped spoons.

The appropriate size of cake tin is given with every recipe: However, the variety of sizes available in the shops is enormous for many manufacturers have not yet changed over to metric measurements. If you do not have, or cannot find, the size of tin recommended in the recipe and have to use one that is slightly different it should not matter too much as long as you watch the cooking time very carefully. The cooking times for the cakes are given as accurately as possible, but all ovens are different which makes it impossible to be exact.

Butter is listed in the ingredients throughout the book. However, margarine can always be used as a substitute, just make sure that it is of the consistency specified.

# CONTENTS

# Chocolate Cakes

| | |
|---|---|
| Sacher Torte with Raspberries | 58 |
| Rich Chocolate Cake | 61 |
| Devil's Food Cake | 62 |
| Chocolate Wholewheat Slice | 65 |
| Chocolate, Bran and Sultana Cake | 66 |
| Chocolate Fudge Cake | 66 |

# Choux Pastry

| | |
|---|---|
| Choux Pastry | 85 |
| Profiteroles | 86 |
| Savoury Profiteroles | 86 |
| Gâteau St. Honoré | 88 |
| Eclairs | 90 |
| Cream Puffs | 91 |

# Meringues & Whisked Cakes

| | |
|---|---|
| Meringues | 69 |
| Pavlova | 70 |
| Coffee and Brown Sugar Meringues | 71 |
| Whisked Sponge | 72 |
| Genoese Sponge Cake | 74 |
| American Brownies | 75 |
| Cherry and Praline Gâteau | 76 |
| Lemon Sponge | 79 |
| Strawberry Roulade | 80 |
| Chocolate Roulade | 81 |
| Brown Bread Roulade | 82 |
| Vanilla Party Sponge | 83 |

# Biscuits

| | |
|---|---|
| Brandy Snaps | 92 |
| Langues de Chat | 95 |
| Chocolate Iced Almond Biscuits | 96 |
| Délices d'Orange | 96 |
| Chocolate Refrigerator Biscuits | 99 |
| Almond Refrigerator Biscuits | 99 |
| Chocolate Chip Cookies | 100 |
| Spiced Cookies | 100 |
| Shortbread | 101 |
| Grasmere Shortcake | 102 |
| Millionaire's Shortbread | 103 |
| Gingerbread Men | 104 |
| Uncooked Chocolate Biscuit Cake | 105 |
| Digestive Biscuits | 106 |
| Oatcakes | 106 |
| Cheese Straws | 108 |
| Beaten Biscuits | 109 |
| Parmesan and Anchovy Thins | 110 |
| Gruyère and Bacon Slices | 110 |

# Tea Time Cakes

No village flower show is complete without a competition for the lightest Victoria Sponge with the best texture and flavour for it is the great cake British kitchen.

Using a Magimix and the 'all-in-one' method it is easy to make one that would stand up to stiff competition. However, there are two rules that have to be followed; indeed these rules are cardinal and applicable to practically every cake in this book.

You must use very soft butter, so soft that it will just drop off the spoon. In all but the hottest weather, the butter should be left in an airing or hot cupboard to soften up. If you forget to take the butter from the fridge until the last minute all is not lost, for you can soften it by chopping it into cubes, leaving it in a low oven for 10 minutes, and then processing it for a few seconds to obtain the right consistency. This also applies if you are using soft margarine, for it needs to be of the same extra soft consistency. Melted butter, on the other hand, just does not work and, with apologies to A. P. Herbert, you want to have it 'Fluffy' just fluffy with no bits at all'.

The other golden rule for 'all-in-one' Magimix cakes is to process them for the shortest possible time. You need to have the cake just mixed, but no more, or it will start to become heavy. This is why you need to use very soft butter, for if you can mix the cake in 7 seconds the result will be that much better than one that takes 15 seconds.

We have taken step-by-step photographs showing how easy and quick it is to make a Victoria Sponge and following the rules of soft butter and minimum processing time you should have no difficulty with any of the other cakes in this book.

## Victoria Sponge Sandwich Cake

8 oz (225 g) self-raising flour
8 oz (225 g) caster sugar
8 oz (225 g) soft butter
4 eggs
A few drops vanilla essence

Prepare two 8″ (20 cm) sandwich tins by greasing them and bottom lining them with silicone paper or greased greaseproof paper. Set the oven to heat to Mark 4, 350°F, 175°C.

If the butter needs softening start by processing it for a few seconds in the Magimix until it reaches the right consistency and then continuing by adding all the other ingredients. Otherwise, start by putting the flour and sugar into the Magimix and processing them together for 4–5 seconds to mix them and give them some aeration. Continue by adding all the other ingredients and processing for 4 seconds. Stop the machine and using a spatula scrape down the sides of the bowl before processing for a further 3 seconds. Check that the cake is fully mixed and if there are still some lumps of butter process again for another 3 seconds to mix them in. Divide the mixture between the two prepared tins, spread it level and bake the cakes for 25 to 30 minutes. The cakes will be cooked when they are golden brown, are springy when you touch the tops and when they have started to shrink from the sides of the tins. On taking them from the oven leave them for about five minutes before turning them out onto a cake rack to cool. Wait until they are completely cold before filling them.

The photographs show the cakes being filled with strawberries and whipped cream, but you can, of course, fill them or flavour them in many different ways. Try strawberry jam and cream or strawberry jam on its own. Leave out the vanilla essence, add some lemon zest to the cake mixture and then fill it with a lemon

Adding the eggs to all the other ingredients for an all-in-one Victoria Sponge.

Stopping the Magimix to scrape down half way through processing the cake.

Turning the mixture into sandwich tins.

Finishing the cake.

butter cream. For a chocolate sponge replace a tablespoonful of flour with a tablespoonful of cocoa and then fill the cake with a chocolate butter cream. The variations are endless, and provided that you stick to the same basic recipe you can experiment with many different flavours.

---

## Oil Based Victoria Sandwich Cake

*This Victoria Sandwich is made with sunflower or groundnut oil. I don't think it is as good as one made more traditionally with butter, but I give the recipe for it could be of use to anybody who has to watch the cholesterol in their diet.*

Set the oven to heat at Mark 4, 350°F, 175°C and grease and bottom line two 7″ (18 cm) sandwich tins.

Put the flour, sugar and baking powder into the Magimix and process for 5 seconds to mix and aerate them. Add all the remaining ingredients and process for 4 seconds. Stop the motor and scrape down before processing for a further 3–4 seconds or until the cake is just mixed. Turn it into the tins and bake it for 30–35 minutes or until golden brown and springy to the touch. Leave the cakes in the tins for three minutes or so before turning them onto a wire rack to cool. Sandwich them together with jam, jam and cream, fresh fruit or any cake filling you like.

5 oz (125 g) self raising flour
5 oz (125 g) caster sugar
1 teaspoon baking powder
2 eggs
7 tablespoons (105 ml) sunflower or groundnut oil
3 tablespoons (45 ml) milk
$\frac{1}{2}$ teaspoon vanilla essence

13

# Coffee Walnut Cake

4 oz (100 g) walnut pieces
3 oz (75 g) caster sugar
3 oz (75 g) self raising flour
3 eggs
2 teaspoons instant coffee
2 tablespoons sunflower or
  corn oil
1 teaspoon baking powder

## Filling

1½ oz (40 g) soft butter
4 oz (100 g) icing sugar
1 teaspoon instant coffee
  dissolved in one teaspoon
  boiling water

*This cake is made with oil rather than butter and needs processing for a very short time indeed. The walnuts give it a distinctive taste and bite, but it is quite rich.*

Pre-heat your oven to mark 4, 350°F, 175°C and grease and bottom line two 7″ (18 cm) sandwich tins.
Process the walnuts for 5–8 seconds or until they are fairly finely chopped. Add all the other ingredients and process for 3 seconds before stopping to scrape down. Process for a further 3–5 seconds or until the cake is just mixed. Pour the mixture into the prepared tins, level the tops and bake for 20 to 25 minutes or until the cakes are lightly browned and shrinking from the sides of the tins. After removing them from the oven leave the cakes in the tins for two or three minutes before turning them out onto wire racks to cool.

Put all the ingredients into the Magimix and process for a few seconds or until they are well mixed. You may have to stop a couple of times to scrape down the bowl. Sandwich the cakes together with the filling and dust the top with icing sugar.

If you can find them decorate the top with chocolate coffee beans or otherwise chocolate or coffee Smarties would look nice.

# Almond Cake

*I always thought that pastry cooks and pâtissiers came from northern Europe and, in particular Paris and northern France, but this almond cake is known in French as Pain de Gênes or Genoa Bread and presumably a Genoese sponge cake also has its provenance in Genoa. I can't find any reason why Genoa should have produced two classic French cakes, but you will find both these cakes in any French cookery book.*

Set the oven to Mark 3, 325°F, 160°C and grease and line a 7″ (18 cm) sandwich tin.

Put the almonds into the Magimix and process them for one minute or until they are very finely ground. Add the flour and sugar and process all three ingredients together for a further 15 seconds.

Add the butter, eggs and Kirsch or orange juice and process for 4 seconds. Stop the machine, scrape down and process for a further 3–4 seconds or until the cake is just mixed. Pour it into the prepared tin, it will be of a fairly liquid consistency, and sprinkle the almonds and then the icing sugar over the top. Bake the cake for an hour, or until a skewer plunged into the centre comes out clean, then leave it in the tin for a few minutes before carefully transferring it to a rack to cool.

3 oz (75 g) almonds
2 oz (50 g) self raising flour
5 oz (150 g) caster sugar
4 oz (100 g) soft butter
3 eggs
2 tablespoons Kirsch or orange juice

**Topping**
1 oz (25 g) flaked almonds
2 teaspoons icing sugar

# Soaked Lemon Cake

*This type of cake, which has lemon juice poured over it after baking, is very popular at the moment and many books give a recipe for one. I find that using a proportion of cornflour gives a texture that is particularly suitable, for the lemon juice soaks in well but does not leave an over-soggy cake.*

6 oz (175 g) self-raising flour
3 oz (75 g) cornflour
8 oz (225 g) caster sugar
1 teaspoon baking powder
Zest of a large lemon
8 oz (225 g) soft butter
4 eggs

**Topping**
6 tablespoons fresh lemon juice
4 tablespoons caster sugar

Set the oven to heat Mark 4, 350°C, 175°F and grease and bottom line an 8″ (20 cm) cake tin.

Put the dry ingredients and the lemon zest into the Magimix and process for 5 seconds to mix and aerate them. Add the butter and eggs and process for a further 5 seconds, then stop the machine, scrape down and process again until the cake is just mixed, which will take from 3 to 5 seconds. Spoon the mixture into the prepared tin and bake it for 25–30 minutes or until it is springy to the touch and the sides have started to shrink from the sides of the tin.

While it is cooking set a small saucepan containing the lemon juice and sugar over a low heat, stir until the sugar has dissolved, then keep it on one side until needed.

On removing the cake from the oven leave it to cool for about three minutes before turning it upside down onto a cake rack. Immediately prick all over the bottom with a skewer or a long pronged fork and then slowly pour or spoon over half the lemon mixture.

Leave it to soak in for a couple of minutes before turning the cake over and repeating the process with the top.

Pricking the cake and spooning on the lemon juice.

Coconut and Rice Cake and Soaked Lemon Cake.

*Coconut is something that people either love or loathe and as this cake contains quite a high proportion of it I would only recommend it to the 'love' brigade. The rice blends well with the coconut and makes a good textured cake that keeps well.*

Grease a 7″ (18 cm) cake tin and then line the bottom and sides with greaseproof or silicone paper. If you use greaseproof paper brush over the inside with melted butter. Set the oven to heat to Mark 4, 350°F, 175°C.

Put the rice, coconut and 3 oz (75g) of the sugar into the Magimix and process for 5 seconds to mix them together. Add the butter, lemon zest and egg yolks, process for 3 seconds then stop and scrape down the bowl before processing for a further 3 seconds or until the ingredients are just mixed. Transfer the cake mixture to a large mixing bowl.

Using a clean, dry bowl, fit the Magimix Whisk and whisk the egg whites for $1\frac{1}{2}$– 2 minutes or until they are stiff. Add the remaining sugar and whisk for a further 20 seconds to incorporate it. Use a metal spoon to gently fold the two mixtures together then spoon it into the tin and bake it for 35–40 minutes or until a skewer plunged into the centre comes out clean. Leave the cake to cool in the tin for ten minutes before turning it out onto a wire rack.

# Coconut and Rice Cake

5 oz (150 g) ground rice
2 oz (50 g) dessicated coconut
6 oz (175 g) caster sugar
4 oz (100 g) soft butter
Zest of a lemon
4 eggs, separated

# Seed Cake

*An old fashioned cake that always arouses interest for it is very definitely liked by some but disliked by others. This is a cake that keeps well and is probably all the better for a couple of days wrapped in foil and stored in a tin.*

2 oz (50 g) almonds
6 oz (175 g) self raising flour
6 oz (175 g) caster sugar
6 oz (175 g) soft butter
3 eggs
½ teaspoon baking powder
3 teaspoons caraway seeds
3 tablespoons sweet sherry or
    milk or a combination of both

Grease and bottom line a 7″ (18 cm) cake tin and set the oven to heat at Mark 3, 325°F, 160°C.

Process the almonds in the Magimix for about 30 seconds or until they are ground. Add the remaining ingredients and process for 5 seconds. Stop and scrape down before processing for a further 3–4 seconds to finish mixing the cake. Turn the mixture into the tin and bake for 1¼ hours or until the cake starts to shrink from the sides of the tin. Leave it to cool for a few minutes before turning it out onto a wire rack. Wait until it is completely cold before storing it.

*This cake has, over the last few years, gone through a tremendous vogue in America and on crossing the Atlantic a version of it was even taken up by the wives at Ambridge. To my mind it is an acquired taste and is best eaten spread with jam. It is slightly spicy and not very sweet, but the courgettes do make it very moist.*

# Courgette Cake

Set the oven to heat at Mark 4, 175°C, 350°F and well oil a 2 lb loaf tin.

Put the walnuts in the Magimix and process them using the pulse for about 5 seconds or until they are coarsely chopped. Remove them and keep them on one side. Fit the grating disc, top and tail the courgettes, cut them to fit the feed tube lengthwise and grate them. Likewise, remove them and keep them on one side.

Dry out the Magimix bowl, change back to the double-bladed knife and add all the remaining ingredients. Process for 5 seconds before stopping to scrape down the bowl. Process for a further 3–5 seconds or until the ingredients are mixed. Add the walnuts and the grated courgettes and use the pulse a few times to just mix them in.

Pour the mixture into the prepared tin and bake for about 1½ hours or until a skewer plunged in the centre comes out clean. Leave the cake in the tin for ten minutes or so before turning it out onto a wire rack to cool.

4 oz (100 g) walnuts
12 oz (350 g) firm courgettes
6 fl oz (180 ml) vegetable oil
2 eggs
4 oz (100 g) plain flour
3 oz (75 g) wholemeal flour
8 oz (225 g) light soft brown
  sugar
1½ teaspoons baking powder
1 teaspoon bicarbonate of soda
1 teaspoon ground cinnamon
1 teaspoon grated nutmeg

The courgettes ready to be pulsed into the cake mixture.

19

# Runny Honey Loaf

3 oz (75 g) hazelnuts
4 oz (100 g) plain flour
1 teaspoon bicarbonate of soda
2 oz (50 g) demerara sugar
½ teaspoon ground cinnamon
½ teaspoon mixed spice
3 tablespoon sunflower oil
2 tablespoons milk
3 tablespoons runny honey
1 egg
3 oz (75 g) sultanas
2 tablespoons runny honey
  for the top

*This is an excellent cake for those who are worried about cholesterol for it is made with an oil mixture and uses only one egg. The use of honey will also please the health food brigade.*

Heat the oven to Mark 3, 325°F, 160°C. Spread the hazelnuts out on a baking sheet, put them in the oven for ten minutes, then rub them in a clean tea towel to remove the skins.

Re-set the oven to Mark 2, 300°F, 150°C and oil a 1 lb (450 g) loaf tin.

Put the hazelnuts into the bowl and process using the pulse or on-off method until they are coarsely chopped. Remove and keep them on one side.

Place the flour, bicarbonate of soda, sugar and spices in the bowl and process for 5 seconds to mix and aerate them. Add the oil, milk, honey and egg and process for 3–5 seconds or until mixed. Finally add the sultanas and approximately 2 oz (50 g) of the hazelnuts and just flick the Magimix on a couple of times to mix them in.

Pour the mixture, which will be very runny, into the loaf tin and bake for half-an-hour. Lower the temperature to Mark 1, 275°F, 140°C and bake for a further hour or until a skewer plunged into the centre comes out clean.

Leave the cake in the tin for five minutes or so before turning it out onto a wire rack to cool. Warm the 2 tablespoons of honey in a small saucepan and dribble about half of it onto the still warm cake. Scatter the remaining nuts over the top and hold them in place by dribbling the remaining honey over them.

# Swiss Roll

4 oz (100 g) self raising flour
4 oz (100 g) caster sugar
½ teaspoon baking powder
2 oz (50 g) soft butter
2 eggs
1 tablespoon milk
A few drops of vanilla essence

*This is a sponge swiss roll and does not, like the roulades in the chapter on the Magimix whisk have whisked egg white folded into it. To keep it really light it does need processing for the shortest possible time and I find that the method below works very well.*

Set the oven to Mark 6, 400°F, 200°C. Grease a swiss roll tin of approximately 8 × 12″ (20 × 30 cm) and line it with a large sheet of silicone paper or greased greaseproof paper.

Put the flour, sugar and baking powder into the Magimix and process for 5 seconds to mix and aerate them. Then add the butter, cut into very small lumps, the eggs, the milk and vanilla essence and using the pulse switch, or on/off method give six very quick bursts on the motor. Stop and scrape down and then give four more bursts. Look at the mixture and if it still has any large lumps of butter use the pulse switch twice more. Turn the mixture into the prepared tin and spread it level, it will make a very thin layer. Put it in the oven and bake it for 10–12 minutes by which time it should have puffed up considerably and the top will be golden brown.

While it is in the oven put the jam, in its pot, in a saucepan of simmering water to heat up and prepare a surface to roll the cake up on.

Lay a tea towel that has been wrung out in very hot water over the work surface and cover it with a large sheet of greaseproof paper. Then sprinkle caster sugar evenly over the paper. The moment the swiss roll comes out of the oven turn it out onto the greaseproof sheet, peel off the bottom paper and spread the warm jam over the inside surface. Using the greaseproof paper carefully roll up the cake and then use the paper to help you roll it onto a plate. It does not matter too much if it cracks, for that will mean that you have a very light sponge.

**Filling**
4 oz (100 g) jam
2 oz (50 g) caster sugar

# Sticky Ginger Cake

*A good old fashioned ginger cake which keeps beautifully and indeed should be kept for a day or so before cutting. If you like a really gooey cake take it out of the oven a few minutes early. One of the easiest ways to weigh out the treacle and syrup is to well cover the pan of your scales with flour which will help to stop the syrups sticking.*

8 oz (225 g) plain flour
4 oz (100 g) soft dark brown sugar
1½ teaspoons ground ginger
3 tablespoons milk
½ teaspoon bicarbonate of soda
4 oz (100 g) soft butter
2 eggs
8 oz (225 g) black treacle
2 oz (50 g) golden syrup
5 knobs stem ginger
3 oz (75 g) sultanas
1 tablespoon chunky marmalade

Grease and bottom line an 8″ (20 cm) cake tin and set the oven to Mark 3, 325°F, 160°C.

Put the flour, sugar and ground ginger into the Magimix and process them for 5 seconds to mix and aerate them. In a small saucepan bring the milk to blood heat and stir in the bicarbonate of soda. Add the milk mixture, butter, eggs, black treacle and golden syrup to the Magimix bowl and process for 5 seconds. Scrape down the sides of the bowl and add the preserved ginger, with the syrup drained off and each knob cut into about five pieces, the sultanas and the marmalade. Pulse the Magimix about half a dozen times to mix everything in, then pour it all into the prepared tin. Bake for one hour, then turn the oven down to Mark 2, 300°F, 150°C, cover the cake with a piece of greaseproof paper and bake for a further 45 minutes or until a skewer plunged into the centre comes out clean. Leave the cake for five minutes before turning it out onto a rack to cool.

# Spiced Golden Syrup Loaf

*This cake has no sugar and is sweetened with golden syrup which makes it very moist. It keeps well and is at its best if left for a day or so before cutting. You can, if you like, reduce the amount of ginger, but I think it needs some spices to counteract the slightly cloying taste of the syrup.*

6 oz (175 g) self raising flour
2 teaspoons ground ginger
½ teaspoon mixed spice
1 teaspoon bicarbonate of soda
4 oz (100 g) golden syrup
3 oz (75 g) butter
6 fl oz (180 ml) milk
1 egg

Set the oven to Mark 3, 325°F, 160°C and grease the bottom line a 1 lb (450 g) loaf tin.

Place the flour, ginger, mixed spice and bicarbonate of soda into the bowl and process for 5 seconds to mix and aerate them.

Measure the syrup into a saucepan. This can be done either by weighing the empty saucepan and then adding the right amount of syrup, or by warming the syrup tin and pouring the syrup directly into the well-floured pan of your scales. Add the butter to the saucepan and heat gently, until the butter has melted. Pour in the milk and stir to mix it in.

Add the egg to the bowl, start the processor and quickly pour the syrup mixture in through the feed tube. Stop the machine to scrape down and process again for a further 2 or 3 seconds. You will then have a very liquid mixture which can be poured into the prepared loaf tin. Put it into the pre-heated oven and bake it for 1¼ hours or until it is shrinking from the sides of the tin and a skewer plunged in the middle comes out clean.

Cool for a few minutes before turning it on to a wire rack.

Yorkshire Parkin and Sticky Ginger Cake.

# Yorkshire Parkin

*This cake keeps well and should in fact be kept for at least three days wrapped in foil before you cut it. This helps the moisture to develop. If you like a strong ginger taste you could add an extra half teaspoon of the ground ginger, but keep the cinnamon which gives it a nice spicy taste.*

6 oz (175 g) black treacle
4 oz (100 g) golden syrup
4 oz (100 g) lard
2 oz (50 g) butter
4 fl oz (120 ml) milk
1 teaspoon bicarbonate of soda
6 oz (175 g) plain flour
6 oz (175 g) medium oatmeal
2 oz (50 g) soft light brown sugar
1 teaspoon ground ginger
$\frac{1}{2}$ teaspoon ground cinnamon

Set the oven to Mark 3, 325°F, 160°C and grease and bottom line a rectangular tin of about 10½ × 7″ (25 × 18 cm).

Put the treacle, golden syrup, lard and butter into a small saucepan, set it over a low heat and stirring occasionally leave it until the fats have melted.

In a separate saucepan add the bicarbonate of soda to the milk and bring it to blood heat for the bicarbonate of soda to dissolve.

Meanwhile put the flour, oatmeal, sugar, ground ginger and ground cinnamon into the Magimix and process them for about 5 seconds so that they are mixed and aerated. Then with the motor working quickly pour the treacle and fat mixture in through the feed tube followed immediately by the warm milk. Stop the machine, scrape down, and then process again for another 2 seconds. Pour the mixture, which will be very runny, into the prepared tin and bake it for about 45 minutes, until the top is a nice brown and a skewer plunged into the centre comes out clean. Leave it in the tin for five minutes before turning it out onto a rack to cool.

When the cake is cold wrap it in foil and keep it from three days to a week before you cut it.

# Strawberry Shortcake

4 oz (100 g) plain flour
3 oz (75 g) wholemeal flour
2 teaspoons baking powder
2 tablespoons caster sugar
¼ teaspoon salt
2 oz (50 g) butter
¼ pint (150 ml) single cream
  or milk

## Filling
Butter for spreading
¼ pint (150 ml) double cream
2 oz (50g) caster sugar
12 oz (350 g) strawberries

*Strawberry shortcake is another import from the other side of the Atlantic and, indeed, no self-respecting American cookbook would be complete without a recipe for it. The shortcake, which is quick and easy to make, is very like a British scone and, in just the same way, is buttered before being filled.*

Set the oven to heat to Mark 7, 425°F, 225°C and grease and lightly flour a baking sheet.

Put the flours, baking powder, sugar and salt into the Magimix and process for a few seconds to mix and aerate them. Add the butter, which has been cut into cubes and process for a further 5 seconds, then with the machine running pour the cream or milk in through the feed tube. Stop the machine almost immediately and scrape the dough, which will be very soft and sticky, out onto a floured board. Flour your hands and use them to roll it into a sausage with a diameter of about 3″ (8 cm). Cut the sausage into eight rounds and bake them for 10–12 minutes or until they have risen and are golden.

While they are still warm split them in two and spread the bottom half with butter and then leave them until they are completely cold before filling.

Whip the cream, this can be done very quickly if you use the Magimix whisk, and fold in the sugar. Reserve eight strawberries for decoration and slice the rest. If you have a 4 mm slicing disc you can do this in the Magimix but only put very light pressure on the pusher.

Fill the shortcakes with the sliced strawberries and a spoonful of cream. Finally decorate the top with a dollop of cream and a strawberry.

Cutting the shortcakes from the roll of dough.

# Apple Upside-down Cake

*This cake doesn't look as beautiful as the American upside-down pineapple cake but I found that one left on the side in my kitchen disappeared with great rapidity. When it is fresh it is very sticky and is probably better eaten with a fork, but it will firm up if you keep it for a day or so. It also makes a good Sunday lunch pudding when it can be eaten warm with large dollops of whipped cream.*

1 lb (450 g) cooking apples
3 tablespoons golden syrup
2 oz (50 g) butter
4 oz (100 g) self raising flour
3 oz (75 g) caster sugar
$\frac{1}{4}$ teaspoon baking powder
$\frac{1}{4}$ teaspoon ground ginger
$\frac{1}{4}$ teaspoon ground cinnamon
2 tablespoons golden syrup
3 oz (75 g) soft butter
2 eggs

Grease an 8″ (20 cm) round cake tin and carefully line the bottom with silicone paper so that it sticks up and covers the sides by about $\frac{1}{2}$″ (1.25 cm).

Peel and core the apples, put them through the 4 mm slicing disc and arrange them on the bottom of the prepared cake tin. Put the 3 tablespoons of golden syrup and the butter in a pan, set it over a low heat and stir until the butter has just melted. Pour this mixture over the apples.

Set the oven Mark 4, 350°F, 175°C.

Put the remaining dry ingredients into the Magimix bowl (which need not have been washed) and process them for 5 seconds to mix and aerate them.

Add the 2 tablespoons of golden syrup, the butter and eggs and process for 5 seconds, stop and scrape down and process for another 3–5 seconds or until the cake is just mixed. Pour the cake into the tin and bake it for about 30 minutes, or until a skewer plunged into the cake part comes out clean and the cake is shrinking from the sides of the tin. Leave it in the tin for at least ten minutes before turning it out and carefully peeling off the silicone paper.

# Apple Cake

*A West country speciality which can be eaten hot with clotted cream or cold spread with butter. I have given instructions for baking it in a square tin, but if you don't happen to own one a round 8" (20 cm) would do just as well.*

Well grease and bottom line a 7" (18 cm) square cake tin and set the oven to Mark 3, 325°F, 160°C.

Peel and core the apples, put them through the slicer, then keep them until needed in a bowl of cold salted water.

Put the flours, sugar and baking powder into the Magimix and process them for 5 seconds. Add the butter, eggs and honey and process for a further 5 seconds. Stop and scrape down the bowl before processing for another 3–5 seconds or until the cake is just mixed.

Drain the apple slices, dry them in a clean tea towel, add half of them to the cake mixture and use the pulse a few times in very quick bursts to just mix them in. Turn the mixture into a bowl, use a spoon to mix in the remaining apple slices and then spoon it into the prepared tin, flatten the top with a spatula, sprinkle over the extra ounce of sugar and bake it for 50–60 minutes or until a skewer plunged in the centre comes out clean.

1 lb (450 g) cooking apples
4 oz (100 g) self raising flour
4 oz (100 g) wholewheat flour
4 oz (100 g) light soft brown sugar
½ teaspoon baking powder
4 oz (100 g) soft butter
2 eggs
1 tablespoon runny honey
1 oz (25 g) light soft brown sugar (for the top)

Five stages in making the Apple Upside-down Cake.

27

# Fruit Cakes & Buns

*Dried fruit now frequently comes in metric packets of 250 g which accurately translates into 8.82 oz. It seems to me that endless remains of 0.82 oz of dried fruits are completely useless so the imperial version of this cake is measured in 8.82 oz or, in other words, just throw in the whole packet!*

This recipe makes a good rich Christmas cake, but as the fruit has been soaked you will find that the finished result is extra moist and therefore will need very careful handling when it comes out of the oven.

The recipe is followed by Magimix recipes for Almond Icing and Royal Icing, but I have not gone into decorating details as these can be found in many other books.

Do try to remember to put the fruit to soak the evening before you intend to bake the cake, for it is well worth while.

The day before you plan to bake the cake: Process the almonds for about 10 seconds or until they are 'nibbed' and turn them into a large mixing bowl. Add the cherries, cut in quarters, the dried fruits, the mixed peel and the zest of the lemons. Put the lemon juice, cider or orange juice in a small saucepan over a low heat, add the black treacle and stir until it has dissolved. Stir in the brandy, rum or rose water and pour the lot over the fruit. Stir well, cover the bowl with a cloth and leave it to soak, overnight or up to 24 hours. Try to stir it a few times while it is soaking.

The next day: Heat the oven to Mark 3, 325°F, 160°C. Butter and line an 8″ (20 cm) cake tin, then put a piece of brown paper extending to 2″ (5 cm) above the top of the tin round the outside, tying it on with a piece of string.

Place the flour, sugar and mixed spice in the Magimix and process for 5 seconds to mix and aerate them. Add the butter and eggs and process for 5 seconds; stop and scrape down and process for a further 3 to 5 seconds or until the mixture has just amalgamated. Add about a third of the fruit and 'pulse' the motor about half a dozen times to just mix it in. Then turn the mixture into the bowl containing the rest of the fruit and use a large wooden spoon to stir the fruit in.

Spoon the cake mixture into the prepared tin, flatten the top with a spoon and bake for two hours and then turn the heat down to Mark 2, 300°F, 150°C and bake for a further 1½ – 2 hours or until a skewer pushed into the centre comes out clean.

Leave the cake in the tin for a few minutes before turning it out onto a wire cake rack. When it is completely cold wrap it in cling film and then foil and store it in a dry, dark cupboard.

## Christmas Cake

2 oz (50 g) almonds
4 oz (100 g) glacé cherries
8.82 oz (250 g) sultanas
8.82 oz (250 g) raisins
8.82 oz (250 g) currants
4 oz (100 g) mixed peel
Zest and juice of 2 lemons
5 fl oz (150 ml) cider or orange juice
1 tablespoon black treacle
5 fl oz (150 ml) brandy, rum, rose water or any mixture
8 oz (225 g) plain flour
8 oz (225 g) soft brown sugar
1 teaspoon mixed spice
8 oz (225 g) soft butter
4 eggs

# Almond Paste

*I like to make my own marzipan and in general I find that whole almonds are moister and have a better taste than bought ground almonds. This recipe makes enough to generously cover the Christmas cake.*

10 oz (275 g) whole blanched
    almonds
10 oz (275 g) caster sugar
1 egg
1 dessertspoon lemon juice

Put the almonds and the sugar into the bowl and process for 1 to 1½ minutes stopping every now and again to check the texture. You need to continue until the almonds are very finely ground and the whole mixture is very smooth. When you reach the smooth stage add the egg and lemon juice and continue processing until the mixture forms a ball. You may need to correct the consistency by the addition of extra lemon juice or sugar. Turn the almond paste onto a board dusted with icing sugar and form it into a ball. Wrap it in cling film and refrigerate until needed.

Almond Paste.

# Royal Icing

2 egg whites
1 lb 4 oz (575 g) icing sugar
1 tablespoon lemon juice
1 teaspoon glycerine

Process the egg whites for 15 seconds or until they are frothy. Add the sugar, lemon juice and glycerine and process for another 10 seconds. Check the consistency and, if necessary, correct it with more sugar or a few more drops of lemon juice. Spread it over the cake with a palette knife and either rough it up or use some in a piping bag to decorate the cake.

Glaze the cake with apricot jam before covering with Almond Paste.

Royal Icing should be used quickly as it may dry and harden.

*Another fruit cake that keeps well and is perfect for family weekends or holidays. Like the Christmas cake, you need to remember to put the fruit to soak for several hours or overnight.*

# Whisky Soaked Fruit Cake

Put the raisins in a small bowl with the whisky and leave them to soak for at least 5 hours or preferably overnight.

Set the oven to Mark 4, 350°F, 175°C, and grease and line a 7″ (18 cm) cake tin.

Process the walnuts for 5–10 seconds or until they are coarsely chopped; remove them and reserve.

Process the demerara sugar for 30–40 seconds or until it has the consistency of caster sugar. Add the flour, bicarbonate of soda and spices and process for 5 seconds to mix and aerate the dry ingredients. Cut the lard into lumps, add it, and process for 5 seconds, then add the eggs and any liquid you can drain from the raisins and process for another 10 seconds or until the mixture is smooth. Finally add the raisins and nuts and flick the switch on and off a few times to pulse them in.

Turn the mixture into the prepared tin and bake it for 30 minutes, then turn the oven down to Mark 3, 325°F, 160°C and bake for a further 30 minutes or until a skewer plunged into the centre comes out clean. Leave for a few minutes before turning the cake out onto a wire rack to cool.

8 oz (225 g) raisins
4 tablespoons whisky
4 oz (100 g) walnuts
5 oz (150 g) demerara sugar
6 oz (175 g) wholewheat or
    wholemeal flour
1 teaspoon bicarbonate of soda
$\frac{1}{2}$ teaspoon grated nutmeg
$\frac{1}{2}$ teaspoon ground cinnamon
4 oz (100 g) lard or cooking fat
2 eggs

# Marmalade Fruit Loaf

*A quick easy-to-make family fruit cake which keeps well and is ideal for a picnic. The marmalade and spices really lift it out of the ordinary and you can use any dried fruit you like or have available.*

7 oz (200 g) self raising flour
4 oz (100 g) soft brown sugar
1 teaspoon mixed spice
2 oz (50 g) butter
2 oz (50 g) lard
2 eggs
2 tablespoons marmalade
4 oz (100 g) mixed dried fruit

Preheat oven to Mark 4, 350°F, 175°C, and well grease a 1 lb (450 g) loaf tin. Place the flour, sugar and mixed spice into the bowl and process for 3 seconds. Add the butter, lard, and eggs and process for a further 5 seconds, then stop the machine and scrape down. Spoon in the marmalade and process again until mixed, this should take no more than 5 seconds. Add the dried fruit and process for a further 2 seconds to just mix it in. Turn the mixture into the tin and cook if for about 1¼ hours or until a skewer comes out clean. Leave it in the tin for 5 minutes before turning it out on a rack to cool.

---

# Banana Loaf

*This loaf is a marvellous way of using up over-ripe bananas and seems to be liked by all age groups. However, if you are making it for small children you may prefer to leave the walnuts out. I like to eat it spread with butter or a thin layer of apricot jam, but my children say this is just greedy and they prefer it on its own.*

2 large ripe bananas
8 oz (225 g) self raising flour
6 oz (150 g) caster sugar
3 oz (75 g) soft butter
2 eggs
½ teaspoon baking powder
2 oz (50 g) walnuts (optional)

Well grease a 1½ lb (675 g) loaf tin and set the oven to Mark 4, 350°F, 175°C.

Cut the bananas directly into the Magimix bowl in approximately 1″ (2½ cm) slices and process them for 10–15 seconds or until they are pulped. Add the other ingredients and process for 5 seconds. Stop, scrape down and process again until the cake is just mixed, this should take no more than 5 seconds. Turn the mixture into the prepared tin and bake it for 50 minutes to an hour or until a skewer plunged into the centre comes out clean. Leave it to cool in the tin for a few minutes before turning it out onto a wire rack.

Banana Loaf and Marmalade Fruit Loaf.

*A good basic easy-to-make family fruit cake.*

Set the oven to Mark 3, 325°F, 160°C and grease and line an 8″ (20 cm) cake tin.

Cut the cherries in half and de-stick them by rinsing them in warm water. Leave them to dry on kitchen paper.

Put the sugar in the Magimix and process it for 20–30 seconds or until it is well ground down. Add the flour, butter, eggs and black treacle and process for 5 seconds – stop, scrape down and process for a further 2–3 seconds or until the cake is just mixed. Remove to a bowl and use a spoon to mix in the fruit and cherries.

Turn the cake into the prepared tin and bake it for about 2 hours or until a skewer plunged in the centre comes out clean. Leave the cake for a few minutes before turning it onto a wire rack to cool.

## Tea Time Fruit Cake

4 oz (100 g) glacé cherries
8 oz (225 g) demerara sugar
10 oz (275 g) self raising flour
8 oz (225 g) soft butter
5 eggs
1 tablespoon black treacle
1 lb (450 g) mixed dried fruit

Cherry Cake and Date and Walnut Loaf.

# Date and Walnut Loaf

4 oz (100 g) stoned dates
3 oz (75 g) walnuts
4 oz (100 g) golden syrup
2 oz (50 g) black treacle
3 oz (75 g) butter
5 fl oz (150 ml) milk
1 egg
8 oz (225 g) wholemeal flour
2 teaspoons baking powder
½ teaspoon mixed spice

*Another popular combination and as the dates and walnuts are so easily chopped in the Magimix it is very quick to make. If you have problems measuring the syrups remember that a tablespoon is the equivalent of just about an ounce.*

Well grease a 2 lb (900 g) loaf tin and set the oven to heat at Mark 3, 325°F, 160°C.

Using the double-bladed knife coarsely chop the dates and set them on one side, then do the same with the walnuts.

Put the syrups and butter into a saucepan, set it over a low heat. Stir to melt the butter then leave it on one side to cool a little. After a few minutes pour in the milk, add the egg and stir to mix them in.

Place the flour, baking powder and mixed spice in the Magimix and process for about 5 seconds to mix and aerate them, then, with the machine running pour the syrup and milk

34

mixture in through the feed tube. Process for a further 2–3 seconds before stopping the machine and adding the dates and walnuts. Use the pulse switch, or just flick the machine on three or four times to mix them in.

Pour the mixture into the prepared tin and bake it for about an hour or until a skewer plunged into the centre comes out clean. Leave the loaf in the tin for about ten minutes before turning it onto a wire rack to cool.

If you like a crunchy top brush the still warm loaf with golden syrup and sprinkle it with demerara sugar.

**Topping (optional)**
1 oz (50 g) golden syrup
1 tablespoon demerara sugar

---

# Cherry Cake

*A very traditional cake, not too rich and one that stores well wrapped in foil in a tin.*

Set the oven to Mark 3, 325°F, 160°C, and grease and line an 8″ (20 cm) cake tin.

To avoid the cherries sinking to the bottom of the cake during cooking start by cutting them in half and then rinsing all the syrup off in warm water. Dry them on a kitchen towel.

Process the almonds for about 15 seconds or until they are finely chopped. Add a tablespoonful of flour and process for a further 10 seconds to chop the almonds further, (they want to remain in fine grains, and be coarser than ground almonds).

Add the remaining flour, the baking powder, sugar, butter, eggs, salt, almond essence and milk and process for 5 seconds. Stop and scrape down the sides before processing for a further 3–5 seconds or until the cake is just mixed. Add the cherries and flick the motor on and off a couple of times to mix them in, but not chop them. Transfer the mixture to the tin and sprinkle the granulated sugar over the top. Bake the cake for 1¼–1½ hours or until it has shrunk away from the sides of the tin and a skewer plunged into the middle comes out clean.

To stop it browning too much you will probably need to cover it with foil half way through cooking.

Leave the cake in the tin for 15 minutes before turning it out onto a wire rack to cool.

8 oz (225 g) glacé cherries
2 oz (50 g) almonds
7 oz (200 g) self raising flour
½ teaspoon baking powder
6 oz (175 g) caster sugar
6 oz (175 g) soft butter
3 eggs
pinch salt
¼ teaspoon almond essence
1 tablespoon milk
1 tablespoon granulated sugar

# Crystallized Fruit Cake

*This colourful cake could well be made as a change from the traditional Christmas cake. The sweetness of the fruit is counteracted by using a sharp lemon glaze. The cake in the photographs was made using the mixture of fruits given in the ingredients but provided you use the same weight of fruit you can mix and match as you please. Health food shops are good places to hunt out little packets of fruit.*

2 oz (50 g) glacé cherries
2 oz (50 g) crystallized ginger
2 oz (50 g) crystallized pineapple
1½ oz (40 g) crystallized lemon peel
½ oz (12 g) angelica stick
4 oz (100 g) almonds
4 oz (100 g) self raising flour
6 oz (175 g) soft butter
6 oz (175 g) caster sugar
3 eggs
2 oz (50 g) flaked almonds

Set the oven to Mark 2, 300°F, 150°C and grease and bottom line an 8″ (20 cm) cake tin.

Prepare the fruit for the cake by cutting the glacé cherries in half and everything else into pieces of about the same size.

Put the 4 oz (100 g) almonds in the Magimix and process them for about one minute or until they are finely ground. Add the flour and process them together for another 20 seconds. Then add the butter, sugar and eggs and process for 5 seconds, stop and scrape down and flick the motor on a couple of times to just mix the sides in. Add the fruit and flaked almonds and mix it in by pulsing the motor a couple of times. Pour the mixture into the prepared tin and bake it for about 1½ hours or until a skewer plunged in the centre comes out clean. Leave it in the tin for a few minutes before turning it out onto a rack to cool.

## Topping

1 oz (25 g) crystallized ginger
1 oz (25 g) crystallized pineapple
¾ oz (18 g) crystallized lemon peel
¼ oz (6 g) angelica stick
1 oz (25 g) glacé cherries
1 oz (25 g) flaked almonds
4 oz (100 g) granulated sugar
4 fl oz (120 ml) water
2 tablespoons lemon juice

Cut the fruit up into small cubes and put it into a bowl. Quarter the cherries, add them and the almonds and use a spoon to just mix them together. Make a syrup by putting the sugar and water into a saucepan and stirring over a gentle heat until the sugar has dissolved. Turn up the heat and boil fast for about 8 minutes or until the syrup reaches the 'crack' stage: (320°F, 147°C on a sugar thermometer) but do not let it caremalise. Take it off the heat and carefully, and quickly, for it will spit, pour in the lemon juice. Swirl it round until the liquid has all amalgamated and leave it to cool a little before use.

Using a pastry brush, brush the cool cake with some of the syrup then spoon all the fruit and nuts onto it. Use a spoon to dribble the remaining syrup over the fruit for as well as giving a bright glaze this will hold the fruit in place.

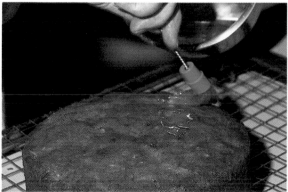

Apricot, Raisin and Yoghurt Loaf.

38

## Apricot, Raisin and Yoghurt Loaf

*This is an unusual combination but it works. The finished result is not too sweet for the taste of the yoghurt really does come through.*

Set the oven to Mark 4, 350°F, 175°C and well grease and bottom line a 1½ lb (675 g) loaf tin.

Slightly warm the yoghurt, stir in the syrup and bicarbonate of soda and leave it to cool.

Process the apricots for about 10 seconds or until coarsely chopped, then remove them and keep them on one side.

Put the flours, baking powder and spice into the bowl and process for 5 seconds to mix and aerate them. Add the butter, eggs and yoghurt mixture and process for another 5 seconds. Stop the machine, scrape down and process for a further 3 seconds before adding the apricots and raisins and using the pulse or on/off method a few times to incorporate them. Turn the mixture into the tin and bake for about 45 minutes or until a skewer pushed into the centre comes out clean. Leave the cake in the tin for a few minutes then turn it onto a wire rack to cool.

5 fl oz (150 ml) plain yoghurt
1 tablespoon golden syrup
1 teaspoon bicarbonate of soda
3 oz (75 g) dried apricots
4 oz (100 g) wholewheat flour
4 oz (100 g) self raising flour
1 teaspoon baking powder
1 teaspoon mixed spice
4 oz (100 g) soft butter
3 eggs
3 oz (75 g) raisins

## Pam's Ovaltine and Fruit Cake

*Pam Brierley, who has done so much work and testing on the cakes in this book, gave me this recipe. It was one of the first cakes she ever made as a child in South Africa and one that she has been making ever since. The Ovaltine gives it an unusual malted flavour that, in fact, combines well with the fruit.*

Set the oven to heat to Mark 4, 350°F, 175°C and grease and line a 1½ lb (675 g) loaf tin.

Put the milk in a saucepan over a low heat, add the bicarbonate of soda and syrup and stir until the syrup has melted.

Put the flour, sugar and Ovaltine in the bowl and process for 5 seconds to mix and aerate them. Pour in the milk mixture and process for a further 5 seconds. Stop and scrape down and, if necessary, process for another 3 seconds. Add the fruit and pulse it in by flicking the motor on about half a dozen times.

Turn the mixture into the tin and bake for 1¼ to 1½ hours or until a skewer plunged into the middle comes out clean. Leave the cake for a minute or two before turning it out onto a wire rack to cool. Slice and serve buttered.

10 fl oz (300ml) milk
½ teaspoon bicarbonate of soda
1 tablespoon golden syrup
12 oz (350 g) plain flour
6 oz (175 g) caster sugar
3 tablespoons Ovaltine
8 oz (225 g) mixed dried fruit

Rock Cakes, Muesli Buns made with molasses sugar and Apricot Buns.

# Muesli Buns

*These are really half way between buns and cookies. They are however, exceedingly easy and quick to make, the mixture just being dropped off a spoon onto the baking sheet. Choose any of the muesli breakfast cereals – I use one that contains lots of fruit and nuts. I also like to make these with the very dark brown unrefined molasses sugar, but if you cannot find it use ordinary soft dark brown sugar.*

4 oz (100 g) butter
4 oz (100 g) self raising flour
3 oz (75 g) dark brown sugar
1 egg
½ teaspoon vanilla essence
6 oz (175 g) muesli cereal

Makes 30–35 buns

Heat the oven to Mark 4, 350°F, 175°C and grease two baking sheets.

Put the butter in a small saucepan and set it over a low heat to melt. Put the flour and sugar in the bowl and process for 5 seconds to mix and aerate them. Add the melted butter, the egg and the vanilla essence and process for a further 5 seconds. Add the muesli cereal and flick the motor on and off, or pulse it, about 5 times to just mix the cereal in.

Using a teaspoon drop the mixture in dollops onto the baking trays. Bake the buns for 8–10 minutes and then remove them with a spatula to a wire tray to cool.

---

## Rock Cakes

*Rock cakes are best if they are eaten really fresh, perhaps while still slightly warm. They can be made with mixed dried fruit but I prefer this version made with sultanas.*

3 oz (75 g) caster sugar
8 oz (225 g) self raising flour
1 teaspoon baking powder
3 oz (75 g) hard butter
1 oz (25 g) lard
1 egg
2 tablespoons milk
3 oz (75 g) sultanas
A little demerara sugar

Set the oven to Mark 6, 400°F, 200°C and well grease two baking sheets.

Put the sugar, flour and baking powder in the bowl together with the roughly chopped butter and lard. Process for 5 seconds then add the egg and milk through the feed tube. Process for no more than 5 seconds or until the mixture starts to amalgamate.

Pour the fruit in through the feed tube and process for a further 2 seconds or until it is just mixed in. Turn the mixture out on to a work surface and use your hands to amalgamate it.

Spoon the mixture into 12 heaps onto the baking sheets and rough them up into a rock shape with a fork. Sprinkle them with a little demerara sugar and bake for 15–20 minutes or until golden brown. Cool them on a wire rack.

---

## Apricot Buns

*These little Apricot Buns are made half and half with self raising and wholewheat flour. The self raising keeps them light and the wholewheat adds a lovely nutty flavour. They are best eaten very fresh, either hot, warm or cold.*

3 oz (75 g) dried apricots
2 tablespoons runny honey
1 oz (25 g) butter
4 oz (100 g) self raising flour
4 oz (100 g) wholewheat flour
2 oz (50 g) light soft brown sugar
1 teaspoon baking powder
1 egg
5 fl oz (150 ml) milk

Makes 15–20 buns

If the apricots are at all hard soak them in the milk for a few hours. However, if they are bright orange and soft they can be used as they are.

Set the oven to Mark 4, 350°F, 175°C and grease two trays of bun tins. Put the honey and butter into a small saucepan and set it over a gentle heat to melt the butter.

If you have soaked the apricots drain them but remember to keep the milk. Place the apricots in the bowl and process for about 10–15 seconds or until they are finely chopped. Add the flours, sugar and baking powder and process for a further 5 seconds to mix them. Add the honey and butter mixture, the egg and the milk and process for a further 5 seconds by which time the buns should be mixed.

Spoon the mixture into the tins and bake the buns for 15–18 minutes or until they are nicely brown on top. Turn them onto a wire rack to cool. These buns are good eaten warm, cut in half and sandwiched with butter or cream cheese.

# Gâteaux, Cheesecakes & Iced Cakes

## Peach Topped Almond Sponge

This is a very moist and light cake and with its cream filling and peach topping you will probably find it easier to eat with a fork. The red-currant jelly not only looks good but adds a welcome sharpness that stops the cake becoming cloying.

Later in the year the cake could be topped with carefully peeled and sliced pears, which would look decorative, and go well with the almonds and redcurrant.

2 oz (50 g) almonds
3 oz (75 g) self raising flour
4 oz (100 g) soft light brown
   sugar
1 teaspoon baking powder
4 oz (100 g) soft butter
2 eggs

Grease and bottom line an 8″ (20 cm) cake tin and heat the oven to Mark 4, 350°F, 175°C.

Put the almonds into the Magimix and process them for about a minute or until they are very finely ground. Add the flour, sugar and baking powder and process for a further 5 to 10 seconds to mix them in. Break in the eggs, add the butter and process for no more than 5 seconds before stopping to scrape down the bowl. Process for a further 5 seconds or until the cake is just mixed.

Turn it into the prepared tin and bake it for about 25 minutes, or until it is well risen, golden brown, and shrinking from the sides of the tin. Leave it in the tin for a few minutes before turning it onto a rack to cool.

Wait until the cake is completely cold before filling and icing it.

### Filling
5 fl oz (150 ml) double cream

Whip the cream until it is stiff. Cut the cake in half, spread on the cream and sandwich the two halves together again.

### Topping
2 peaches
3 tablespoons redcurrant jelly

Heat the redcurrant jelly in a bowl standing over a pan of boiling water. You may find that it does not melt completely and if this happens put it through a small strainer into another bowl and then place that bowl over the hot water.

Spoon about two-thirds of the jelly onto the cake and then using a palette knife, spread it over the top and sides.

While the jelly on the cake is setting prepare the peaches by boiling up a saucepan of water and blanching them for a few seconds so that they can easily be skinned. After skinning cut them in half, remove the stones and slice the halves as evenly as you can. Arrange the slices on top of the cake and using a pastry brush glaze them over with the remaining redcurrant jelly.

# Frosted Walnut Cake

When I was a child one of the great weekend treats was a Fuller's Walnut Cake: A delicious sponge cake sandwiched together with vanilla butter cream and iced with a marvellous white American type frosting. This is my humble attempt to re-create it, and, even if the taste is different, it is good.

I have given instructions for cooking the cakes in 7″ (18 cm) sandwich tins, but this is because I remember the cake as being tall with a smallish diameter and if you wish it would be perfectly alright to use 8″ (20 cm) tins.

The frosting is not made in the Magimix, but I have given the recipe for it because it goes so well with this cake.

Well grease and botton line two 7″ (18 cm) sandwich tins and set the oven to Mark 4, 175°C, 350°F.

Put the walnuts into the Magimix and process them using the pulse switch or by flicking the machine on and off a few times, until they are coarsely chopped. Add all the remaining ingredients, process for 5 seconds, then stop and scrape down the bowl. Process for a further 3–5 seconds, or until the cake is just mixed. Divide the cake mixture between the prepared tins and bake for 25–30 minutes or until the tops are brown and springy to the touch and the cakes are shrinking away from the sides of the tins. Leave them to cool for 5 minutes before turning them out onto a wire rack.

Put the filling ingredients into the Magimix and process them until they are amalgamated and smooth. You might want to taste and perhaps add a little more vanilla essence. Cut each of the cakes in half and using a third of the filling on each layer sandwich them back together again.

Put the sugar, water and egg whites in a bowl set over a saucepan of boiling water and whisk it for several minutes or until the frosting is thick and stands up in peaks. When it is of a spreading consistency spread it over the cake and while it is still soft press on the walnut halves.

2 oz (50 g) walnuts
7 oz (200 g) self raising flour
7 oz (200 g) soft butter
6 oz (175 g) caster sugar
1 tablespoon golden syrup
3 eggs

**Filling**
4 oz (100 g) unsalted butter
6 oz (175 g) icing sugar
½ teaspoon vanilla essence

**Frosting**
8 oz (225 g) granulated sugar
5 fl oz (150 ml) water
2 egg whites
7 walnut halves

One more layer to come!

45

# Passion Cake with Cream Cheese and Orange Frosting

*Carrot Cake, or Passion Cake as it is often more romantically called, I first met in Australia, but I think it can trace its origins to America. It is now frequently found in British delicatessens as well as in many recipe books and I find this version which can be made with either plain or wholemeal flour or a mixture particularly good. I have given a cream cheese and orange frosting, but if you want something less rich you can always serve the cake plain with just a dusting of icing sugar.*

4 oz (100 g) walnuts
8 oz (225 g) peeled carrots
6 oz (175 g) plain or wholemeal flour
8 oz (225 g) caster sugar
1½ teaspoons bicarbonate of soda
1½ teaspoons baking powder
½ teaspoon salt
1½ teaspoons ground cinnamon
8 fl oz (240 ml) sunflower or groundnut oil
3 eggs
1 teaspoon vanilla essence

### Frosting
6 oz (175 g) cream cheese
3 oz (75 g) butter
3 oz (75 g) icing sugar
Zest and juice of an orange

Set the oven to heat to Mark 4, 350°F, 175°C and grease and line an 8″ (20 cm) cake tin.

Process the walnuts for about 5 seconds to roughly chop them and set them on one side. Fit the grating disc, grate the carrots and set them on one side.

Change back to the double-bladed knife and process all the dry ingredients for about 5 seconds to mix and aerate them. Add the oil, eggs and vanilla essence and process for a further 5 seconds before adding the nuts and grated carrot. Use the pulse, or keep switching the machine on and off, to incorporate them. Turn the mixture into the tin and bake it for about an hour or until a skewer plunged into the centre comes out clean.

Leave the cake in the tin for a few minutes before turning it out onto a cake rack. Wait until it is completely cold before filling and icing it.

Put all the frosting ingredients into the bowl and process them for about 10 seconds, stopping once or twice to scrape down the bowl. Refrigerate the frosting for an hour or so before use to let it thicken and harden.

Cut the cake through the middle and sandwich it together with about a third of the frosting. Spread the remainder of the top and sides and use a fork to rough it up and give it a texture.

# Tonilles aux Framboises

4 oz (100 g) shelled hazelnuts
5 oz (150 g) soft butter
3 oz (75 g) caster sugar
6 oz (175 g) plain flour

*The tonilles is really a hazelnut biscuit; it is quite delicious, very suitable for high days and holidays and seems to go particularly well with raspberries. You could try other fruit, peaches are good, and in the winter mangos and paw-paws, peeled, sliced and arranged in stripes would look and taste very exotic.*

Take two sheets of silicone or well greased greaseproof paper and mark a rectangle of approximately 10 × 7″ (25 × 18 cm) on each.

Heat the oven to Mark 3, 325°F, 160°C. Spread the hazelnuts out on a baking sheet and bake them for 10 minutes. Watch them very carefully for they burn easily and may need turning after five minutes or so. Put the hot hazelnuts in a clean tea towel and rub it hard to remove the skin from the nuts; it should flake off quite easily.

Put the hazelnuts into the Magimix and process them for 20 to 30 seconds or until they are finely chopped. Add the butter, sugar and flour, process for 5 seconds, scrape down and process for another 7 seconds or until the dough has amalgamated.

Press half the mixture onto each marked rectangle. You may find it is easier if you use a well floured rolling pin and a sharp knife to even up the edges. Put the prepared mixture, which will be very soft, into the fridge for at least half an hour before baking. Set the oven to Mark 4, 350°F, 175°C and bake the biscuits for 25–30 minutes or until they are lightly coloured. Set the cooked biscuit on a rack to cool, but leave the paper on until you are ready to fill the Tonilles. (The topping and filling are on the next page)

Making the Tonilles.

48

**Topping:**
8–12 oz (225–350 g) fresh
   raspberries
8 oz (225 g) fresh redcurrants
White of an egg
3 oz (75 g) caster sugar

**Filling:**
1 recipe Créme Pâtissiére
   (see page 91)
or 10 fl oz (300 ml) double
   cream (whipped)

To frost the redcurrants put the egg white in a saucer and break it up, until it is liquid, but not frothy, with a fork. Spread the sugar out on a plate and lay out a sheet of silicone or greased greaseproof paper. Hold each bunch of redcurrants by the stalk and roll the fruit round in the egg white. Briefly hold up the stalk for any excess to drain off, then roll it around in the sugar. Carefully pull the frosted stalks on the paper and leave them until they are dry.

Place one of the biscuit rectangles on to a board or serving dish and carefully peel off the paper. Reserve 2 tablespoons of the Créme Pâtissiére or the cream and spread the remainder onto the rectangle but leave a border of about ½″ round the edge. Carefully peel the paper from the other rectangle and using two palette knives, or your hands, very gently place it on top of the cream filling.

Dip the bottom of each raspberry in the reserved cream and place them decoratively in position on top of the Tonilles. Use a teaspoon to smear a small amount of cream onto the cake and fix the redcurrants into position.

Frosting the redcurrants.

*This cheesecake isn't too rich and will keep well. The recipe uses nutmeg and cinnamon but you can replace them with the zest and juice of a lemon.*

Set the oven to Mark 3, 325°F, 160°C and grease and bottom line an 8″ (20 cm) loose bottomed cake tin.

Put the butter in a small saucepan and set it to melt over a low heat. Roughly break up the biscuits and process them to breadcrumb stage, then, with the motor working, pour the butter in through the feed tube. Process for a further 5 seconds then turn the mixture into the prepared tin, spread it out and press it down with the back of a metal spoon.

Crumb the bread by processing it for about 10 seconds then add the cheese, eggs, sugar and spices and process for 5 seconds to mix them in. Add the sultanas and pulse them in by flicking the machine on two or three times. Pour the mixture into the tin and bake it for 45 minutes or until golden brown and springy to the touch. Wait until it is cool before lifting it from the tin and eat it cold.

# Baked Cheesecake

**Base**
2 oz (50 g) digestive biscuits
2 oz (50 g) ginger biscuits
3 oz (75 g) butter

*To much butter for biscuits needs more biscuits*

**Filling**
12 oz (350 g) cottage cheese
2 oz (50 g) white bread (crustless)
3 eggs
3 oz (75 g) sugar
¼ teaspoon grated nutmeg
¼ teaspoon ground cinnamon
2 oz (50 g) sultanas

51

# Pineapple Cheese-cake

*This cheesecake has a marvellous light consistency and can be made equally well with tinned peaches or pears. For my taste tinned fruits are inclined to be oversweet and sticky, but as no extra sugar is added to this filling the whole flavour of the fruit seems to come through. It is extra good if made with the digestive biscuits given on page 106.*

*Pineapple pieces sometimes come in a 16 oz (454 g) cans and if you use one of these you will need to add an extra half teaspoon of gelatine or you may find that it won't set.*

4 oz (100 g) digestive biscuits
2 oz (50 g) melted butter
1 packet gelatine
1 14½ oz (411 g) can pineapple
   pieces
8 oz (225 g) cream cheese
5 fl oz (150 ml) sour cream
2 eggs, separated
Few drops vanilla essence
Zest and juice of ½ a lemon

### For the Top
5 fl oz (150 ml) double cream
A few young mint leaves
   (optional)

Grease and bottom line an 8″ (20 cm) loose-bottomed cake tin. Place the roughly broken up biscuits in the bowl and process until they resemble fine breadcrumbs, then, with the motor working, pour the butter in through the feed tube and continue to process for a few more seconds. Press the biscuit mixture into the prepared tin, smooth it over with a metal spoon and put it in the fridge to chill for about half-an-hour or until it is firm.

**To make the filling**
Take two tablespoons of syrup from the can of pineapple and put it in a small bowl over a saucepan of hot water. Sprinkle over the gelatine and leave it to melt.

Rinse out the Magimix bowl and put in the cream cheese, sour cream, egg yolks, vanilla essence and the lemon zest and juice. Process for about 15 seconds to mix well; you may have to stop once to scrape it down. Add the melted gelatine and, having removed a few pieces of pineapple for decoration, the remaining contents of the pineapple can. Process briefly, (for about 3 or 4 seconds). This should mix everything together without the pineapple being cut up too much.

Carefully wash and dry the Magimix bowl and then fit the egg whisk. When the pineapple mixture is on the point of setting whisk the egg whites until they are stiff. Gently but thoroughly fold the beaten egg whites into the pineapple mixture and then pour the whole into the prepared cake tin and chill until set.

Just before serving remove the cheesecake from the tin, (it will probably be easier to leave it on the base) place it on a plate and decorate the top with the reserved pineapple, whipped cream and, if you have them, a few young mint leaves.

*Another pretty looking cake. The combination of the slightly nutty tasting base, the smooth filling and the rather tart gooseberries is, I think, very good. However, with its three layers it is not as quick to make as some and it does also take a few minutes to top and tail the gooseberries and arrange them on the top. Try to use gooseberries that are reasonably soft for hard 'bullet' ones will take a very long time to cook.*

# Gooseberry Topped Cheesecake

Grease an 8″ (20 cm) cake tin and line the bottom and sides with silicone paper. Set the oven to heat to Mark 5, 375°F, 190°C.

Put all the base ingredients into the Magimix and process for 20–25 seconds. Turn the mixture out, use well floured hands to amalgamate it into a ball, then use your fingers to press it evenly into the bottom of the cake tin. Bake it for ten minutes to just set the base. While it is in the oven prepare the filling by processing all the ingredients together for 10 seconds or so. After the ten minutes baking take the tin from the oven, turn the temperature down to Mark 4, 350°F, 175°C, pour the filling into the cake tin and return it to the oven for 30–35 minutes or until the filling has just set.

While the cheese filling is cooking prepare the gooseberries by topping and tailing them and make the syrup or glaze by putting the water and sugar into a small saucepan and setting it over a low heat. Stir the syrup until it is clear and the sugar has melted then turn up the heat and boil it hard for 4 minutes. Set it on one side to cool a little before you use it.

On removing the cheesecake from the oven turn the temperature down again, this time to Mark 3, 325°F, 160°C. Arrange the gooseberries in circles on top of the cheese mixture and then, using a spoon, dribble the syrup over the top. Return the whole cheesecake to the oven and bake it for 25–30 minutes or until the gooseberries are cooked and soft.

This cheesecake is best if it is eaten slightly warm, but if you plan to eat it cold take it out of the fridge for a couple of hours so that it is served at room temperature.

**Base**
4 oz (100 g) 81% (or wholemeal) flour
2 oz (50 g) caster sugar
3 oz (75 g) butter

**Filling**
8 oz (225 g) cottage cheese
8 oz (225 g) cream cheese
2 eggs
4 oz (100 g) caster sugar
Zest and juice of a lemon

**Topping**
8–12 oz (225–350 g) fresh gooseberries
3 oz (75 g) caster sugar
5 fl oz(150 ml) water

# Lemon Yoghurt Cake

6 oz (175 g) self raising flour
4 oz (100 g) caster sugar
½ teaspoon baking powder
Zest of a large lemon
1 pot, 5 fl oz (150 ml) plain
    yoghurt (less 1 tablespoon for
    icing)
5 fl oz (150 ml) sunflower oil
2 eggs

*This cake, which is slightly sour and very lemony, is very refreshing and quite perfect for a hot summer's day. I have given instructions for baking it in a square tin, chiefly because I think it looks nice, but it is also an easy shape to cut, but if you haven't got one you can always use a 7″ (18 cm) round cake tin.*

Set the oven to Mark 3, 325°F, 160°C and grease and bottom line a 8″ (20 cm) square cake tin.

Put the flour, sugar, baking powder and lemon rind into the Magimix and process them for 3–5 seconds to mix and aerate them. Add the yoghurt, oil and eggs and process for 3–5 seconds to just mix them in. Stop and scrape down and process for another couple of seconds to mix in the edges. Turn the mixture into the prepared tin and bake for 35–40 minutes until the cake is firm to the touch and just starting to shrink away from the sides of the tin. Leave it for a few minutes before turning the cake out onto a wire rack to cool.

# Lemon Yoghurt and Butter Icing

2 oz (50 g) unsalted soft butter
8 oz (225 g) icing sugar
Juice of a lemon
1 tablespoon yoghurt
Zest of a lemon

If you own a zester remove the zest from the lemon in strips and keep them. Otherwise grate the peel, but also keep it.

Put the butter, sugar and lemon juice into the bowl and process for 6–8 seconds, stopping once to scrape down. Then add the yoghurt and process for a further 2–3 seconds. Cut the cold cake in half through the centre and spread the bottom half with a layer of the icing. Sandwich it together again and use the rest of the icing to cover the top and sides. If you then drop the shreds of lemon peel onto the top of the cake, you will find that they will settle into the icing and look very decorative.

# Spicy Orange Cake

*This cake is very moist and has that marvellous slightly bitter taste of orange zest (do not try to economise by using the zest of just one orange) combined with a faint prickle of ginger. I like to make it with wholemeal flour when I add another ½ teaspoon of baking powder, but the finished cake will be slightly lighter if made half-in-half self-raising and wholemeal flour. I fill and ice it with a rather wet butter icing, but if after mixing you put it in the fridge for half an hour or so it should thicken to a spreading consistency.*

Set the oven at Mark 4, 350°F, 175°C, and grease and bottom line two 7″ (18 cm) sandwich tins.

Lemon Yoghurt Cake and Spicy Orange Cake.

Place the flour, sugar, baking powder, orange zest and ginger in the bowl and process them together for about 5 seconds to mix them well. Add the butter and eggs and process for 3 seconds to mix, stop the machine and scrape down and process again for another 2 or 3 seconds, by which time the butter and eggs should be mixed in. Spoon the mixture into the sandwich tins and bake for 20–25 minutes, or until the cake has shrunk from the sides of the tin. Leave the cakes in the tins for a few minutes before turning them onto a rack to cool.

Put all the ingredients in the bowl and process for a few seconds to mix. As this is very liquid you will probably need to stop and scrape the bowl down a couple of times.

Put the icing in the fridge to cool and thicken, then spread half over one of the cakes, place the other cake on top and spread over the remaining icing.

The top looks pretty if decorated by dropping some strands of orange peel onto the icing.

3 oz (75 g) self raising flour and
3 oz (75 g) wholemeal flour or
6 oz (175 g) wholemeal flour and
    and extra $\frac{1}{2}$ teaspoon baking
    powder
6 oz (175 g) light soft brown
    sugar
1 teaspoon baking powder
Zest of 2 oranges
1 teaspoon ground ginger
6 oz (175 g) soft butter
3 eggs

**Filling and Icing**
Juice of one orange
4 oz (100 g) icing sugar
2 oz (50 g) butter

# Chocolate Cakes

## Sacher Torte with Raspberries

6 oz (175 g) plain chocolate
4 oz (100 g) self raising flour
4 oz (100 g) caster sugar
4 oz (100 g) soft butter
4 eggs, separated

**Filling**
5 fl oz pint (150 ml) double cream

**Icing and Topping**
5 fl oz (150 ml) single cream
8 oz (225 g) plain chocolate
8 oz (225 g) raspberries

*A rich Austrian chocolate cake with a chocolate ganache icing; very delicious filled with raspberry jam and eaten as it is. This version with fresh raspberries is sensational both to taste and to look at and is ideal as the centrepiece for a summer birthday or celebration.*

Grease and bottom line two 8″ (20 cm) sandwich tins and set the oven to heat to Mark 4, 350°F, 175°C.

Place the chocolate in a bowl set over a saucepan of very hot water. Leave it to melt, stir until it is smooth and then put it on one side to cool a little. Put the flour and sugar in the Magimax and process them for 3–5 seconds to mix them. Add the chocolate, butter and egg yolks and process for a further 5 seconds, or until just mixed. Transfer the mixture to another bowl, carefully wash and dry the Magimix bowl, fit the egg whisk and whisk the egg whites for about 1½ minutes or until they are stiff. Use a metal spoon to fold the beaten egg whites into the chocolate mixture and then divide it between the two prepared tins. Bake the cakes for approximately 25–30 minutes or until a skewer plunged into the centre comes out clean. Leave the cakes to cool in the tins for a few minutes before turning them out onto a rack.

Whip the cream until stiff and when the cakes are completely cold use it to sandwich them together.

For the chocolate ganache icing pour the cream into a small saucepan and bring is slowly to the boil. Take the pan off the heat, add the broken up chocolate and stir until it has melted. Leave it until the ganache is nearly cold then process it in the Magimix for 10 seconds or so or until it thickens. Using a spatula spread it carefully over the top and sides of the cake saving some for piping on as decoration if you wish. Arrange the raspberries on the top and either leave it plain or pipe on the reserved chocolate icing.

# Rich Chocolate Cake

*A rich chocolate sandwich cake that keeps well and is ideal for a celebration or birthday. You can, if you wish, use ground almonds, but I have given instructions for using whole or flaked almonds. Almonds are easily ground down in the Magimix and the whole or flaked ones do have a very much better and fresher taste than the bought ready ground ones.*

*The almond and chocolate butter cream filling blends well with the cake, but if you want something less rich you could make a double quantity of the glacé icing and use half of it to fill the cake.*

Heat the oven to Mark 3, 325°F, 160°C and grease and bottom line two 8″ (20 cm) sandwich tin.

Put the chocolate, butter and sugar in a saucepan, place it over a gentle heat and stirring occasionally leave until they have just melted.

Place the almonds in the Magimix and process them for a minute or until they are finely ground. Add the flour, cocoa and bicarbonate of soda and process for a further 30 seconds to grind the almonds into the flour. Pour in the melted chocolate mixture, add the eggs and milk, and process for 3 seconds before stopping the machine and scraping down. Process for a further 2 seconds by which time the ingredients should be well amalgamated. Divide the mixture between the two prepared tins and bake for 30 minutes or until the sides start to shrink away from the sides of the tin and the cakes are firm to the touch. Leave them in the tins for five minutes before turning them onto a rack to cool.

Put the almonds into the Magimix and process them for 10–15 seconds or until they are finely chopped. Dissolve the cocoa in the hot water, or rum or brandy, and add it and the butter and icing sugar to the almonds in the bowl. Process for about 5 seconds, stop and scrape down and process for a further 5 seconds or so or until you have a smooth mixture. Use to sandwich the two cakes together.

Toast the almonds to a light brown colour under a hot grill, turning them once. Watch them very carefully for they burn easily.

Dissolve the cocoa in the hot water and put it into the bowl together with the icing sugar. Process for 5–10 seconds or until the icing is smooth. You can adjust the consistency by adding a little more icing sugar or a few drops of water. Spoon it on top of the cake and use a spatula to spread it evenly over the surface. While the icing is still wet arrange the almonds on the top.

4 oz (100 g) plain chocolate
5 oz (150 g) butter
4 oz (100 g) soft light brown sugar
2 oz (50 g) blanched whole or flaked almonds
6 oz (175 g) plain flour
1 oz (25 g) cocoa
2 teaspoons bicarbonate of soda
2 eggs
3 fl oz (90 ml) milk

### Almond and Chocolate Butter Cream Filling
2 oz (50 g) almonds
1 tablespoon cocoa
1 tablespoon hot water (or warmed rum or brandy)
2 oz (50 g) butter
4 oz (100 g) icing sugar

### Chocolate Glacé Icing
1 tablespoon cocoa
1 tablespoon hot water
4 oz (100 g) icing sugar
1 oz (25 g) flaked almonds

# Devil's Food Cake

*This cake is an American classic and is very rich and moist. Many recipes use milk that has been soured with the addition of lemon juice, but I find that the flavour of the lemon fights with the chocolate, so I use yoghurt which seems to work well.*

*I like the addition of sour cream to the filling, but some people prefer to use whipped cream and no extra sugar. The frosting recipe makes quite a large quantity, perhaps rather too much for one cake: However it will keep in the fridge for a week or two or in the freezer for several months.*

8 oz (225 g) self raising flour
2 oz (50 g) cocoa powder
½ teaspoon bicarbonate of soda
10 oz (275 g) caster sugar
4 oz (100 g) softened butter
2 eggs
5 fl oz (150 ml) yoghurt
3 fl oz (90 ml) milk

Set the oven to Mark 4, 350°F, 175°C and grease and bottom line two 9″ (22 cm) sandwich tins.

Put the flour, cocoa powder, bicarbonate of soda and sugar in the bowl and process them for 5 seconds to mix and aerate them. Add the remaining ingredients and process for 3–5 seconds. Stop the motor and scrape down before processing for a further 2–3 seconds or until the cake is just mixed together.

Divide the mixture between the two prepared tins and bake for about 25 minutes or until the tops are just firm to the touch. Leave the cakes in the tins for a few minutes before turning them out to cool on a wire rack.

**Sour Cream Filling**
3 fl oz (90 ml) double cream
3 fl oz (90 ml) sour cream
2 oz (50 g) icing sugar

Use the Magimix Whisk and whisk the double cream until it is thick, add the sour cream and icing sugar and whisk for 3 or 4 seconds to mix them in. Cut each cake in half through the middle and sandwich the layers together with the filling.

**Chocolate Fudge Frosting**
A small can: 6 oz (170 g)
    evaporated milk
8 oz (225 g) granulated sugar
4 oz (100 g) butter
4 oz (100 g) plain chocolate
1 teaspoon vanilla essence

Put the sugar and evaporated milk in a saucepan and place it over a gentle heat. Stir constantly until the sugar has melted, and then turn up the heat and bring the mixture to the boil. Cease stirring and boil for 7 minutes.

Pour the milk and sugar mixture in to Magimix, add the butter, chocolate and vanilla essence and turn the motor on. Continue processing until the mixture is thick and creamy, this will probably take about 30 seconds.

Leave the frosting until it is cold and spread over the top and sides of the cake.

*This chocolate cake, which is American in origin, is ideal for the health food fanatics though they may prefer to forget about the cream and sandwich it together with raspberry jam. It has an unusual texture which contrasts well with the cream filling.*

Set the oven to Mark 4, 350°F, 175°C and grease a 1½ lb (675 g) loaf tin.

Place the flour, sugar, cocoa, cinnamon, orange zest and baking powder in the bowl and process for about 7 seconds to smooth out any lumps in the sugar and to mix and aerate the dry ingredients. Add the remaining ingredients and process for 5 seconds. Stop and scrape down before processing for a further 3 to 5 seconds. Turn into the tin and bake for 25–30 minutes or until the cake feels springy and is coming away from the sides of the tin. Leave it in the tin for a few minutes before turning it onto a wire rack to cool.

Whip the cream until stiff and then stir in the icing sugar and orange curaçao, brandy or orange juice.

Take a very sharp knife and cut the cake in half through the middle. Then extremely carefully cut each half in half again and use two palette knives to separate the halves. Place the bottom half onto a serving plate, spread over a third of the cream and using the palette knives cover it with the next slice. If the middle slices break it does not really matter, just put them together as well as you can. Cover with more cream, then the next slice followed by the rest of the cream and finally the top. Press it down slightly so that the cream starts to ooze out round the edges.

# Chocolate Wholewheat Slice

4 oz (100 g) 100% wholewheat flour
4 oz (100 g) soft brown sugar
2 tablespoons cocoa
½ teaspoon ground cinnamon
Zest of an orange
2½ teaspoons baking powder
4 oz (100 g) soft butter or soft margarine
2 eggs
2 tablespoons orange juice

**Filling**
8 fl oz (240 ml) double cream
2 dessertspoons icing sugar
1 tablespoon orange curaçao, brandy or orange juice

Whipping cream with the Magimix whisk – rather more than needed for this cake!

# Chocolate, Bran and Sultana Cake

1 oz (25 g) bran
4 oz (100 g) sultanas
4 tablespoons fresh or packet orange juice
4 oz (100 g) self raising flour
2 oz (50 g) wholemeal flour
1 oz (25 g) cocoa
2 oz (50 g) demerara sugar
½ teaspoon baking powder
4 oz (100 g) soft butter
2 eggs
1 tablespoon golden syrup

*This is a good tea-time cake that is neither too sweet nor too rich and keeps well.*

Put the sultanas and bran in a small bowl, pour over the orange juice and stir to mix it in. Leave this to soak for half an hour before continuing with the cake.

Grease and bottom line a 1 lb (450 g) loaf tin and set the oven to Mark 3, 325°F, 160°C.

Put the sugar in the Magimix and process for 10 seconds to grind it down a little. Then add the remaining dry ingredients and process them for 5 seconds to mix and aerate them. Add the butter, eggs and golden syrup and process for 5 seconds before stopping to scrape down the bowl. Process for a further 3 seconds then spoon in the bran and sultana mixture and flick the machine on and off a few times or use the pulse to mix it in.

Pour the mixture into the prepared loaf tin and bake it for about an hour or until a skewer plunged into the centre comes out clean. Leave it in the tin for five minutes or so before turning it out onto a rack to cool.

---

# Chocolate Fudge Cake

2 oz (50 g) plain chocolate
5 oz (150 g) self raising flour
1 oz (25 g) cocoa
1 teaspoon baking powder
6 oz (175 g) light soft brown sugar
6 oz (175 g) soft butter
3 eggs
A few drops vanilla essence

*This is my Magimix adaptation of a recipe I cut out of a magazine when I was first married. My ingredients aren't exactly the same but even so in those far off days the approximate cost was given as 4/6d! However it makes a rich gooey cake and it has an icing which matches it perfectly.*

Set your oven to Mark 3, 325°F, 160°C and grease and bottom line an 8″ (20 cm) cake tin.

Put the chocolate in a small basin and stand it over a saucepan of hot water to melt the chocolate.

Put the flour, cocoa, baking powder and sugar in the bowl and process for 5 seconds, then add the butter, eggs and vanilla essence and process for a further 5 seconds. Scrape down, add the melted chocolate and process for a final 5 seconds. Turn into the tin and bake for 1 hour to 1 hour 10 minutes or until the cake is shrinking from the sides of the tin and a skewer plunged into the middle comes out clean. Leave the cake in the tin for five minutes before turning it out onto a rack to cool.

**Icing**

2 oz (50 g) plain chocolate
6 oz (175 g) light soft brown sugar
2 oz (50 g) butter
Zest of an orange

Melt the chocolate in a small bowl over a pan of hot water. Put the sugar, butter and orange zest into the bowl and process for 10 seconds. Stop the motor, add the melted chocolate, and process for a further 5 seconds. Use as required.

Chocolate, Bran and Sultana Cake.

Cut the cake through the middle and spread on about half the icing. Sandwich together and spread the rest over the top, roughing it up with a palette knife or fork. It looks pretty if, when the icing has set, you sprinkle it with icing sugar.

# Meringues & Whisked Cakes

*Meringues are liked by nearly everybody and are very seldom out of place, being suitable for practically every occasion.*

Line two baking sheets with silicone paper or very well greased greaseproof paper and set the oven to heat to Mark ½, 225°F, 110°C.

Fit the Magimix whisk and whisk the egg whites for 1½ to 2 minutes or until they are stiff but not dry. Overwhipped dry egg whites give dry rather chalk like meringues. With the machine running add about ⅓ of the sugar and continue whisking for about 20 seconds or until the mixture is smooth and shiny. Add the remaining sugar and just whisk it in; no more than 5 seconds. Either spoon or pipe the mixture onto the prepared sheets and bake the meringues for 1 to 1½ hours, depending on size, and until they are crisp and light.

## Meringues

4 egg whites
7 oz (200 g) caster sugar

# Pavlova

*A famous Australian use of meringue which has in recent years become very popular over here. Cream and practically any soft fruit can be used to fill it or in winter the chocolate and cream filling used for the Chocolate Roulade (page 82) would be good.*

*A Pavlova is usually cooked at a slightly higher temperature than individual meringues for ideally it should be golden and crisp on the outside and marshmallow like and soft inside. You will find that the cooked pavlova needs careful handling for it will be very fragile and will crack easily.*

4 egg whites
7 oz (200 g) caster sugar
1 teaspoon cornflour
½ teaspoon white wine vinegar

Line two baking sheets with silicone paper and using a plate as a guide draw a circle of approximately 8″ (20 cm) diameter on each sheet. Set the oven to heat to Mark 1, 275°F, 140°C.

Before starting make sure that the Magimix bowl, lid and whisk are scrupulously clean and free from grease.

Whisk the egg whites for 2 minutes or until stiff, but not over stiff and dry. Stop the machine and sprinkle on the cornflour, the vinegar and about ⅓ of the sugar. Whisk for a further 20–25 seconds or until the meringue is smooth and shiny. Add the remaining sugar and whisk for 3–5 seconds to just whisk it in. Spread half the meringue fairly evenly over each of the circles and bake it for about an hour or until it has crisped on the outside. Turn off the oven and leave the meringue until it is cold.

**Filling**
10 fl oz (300 ml) double cream
8 oz (225 g) fresh fruit

About an hour before serving the meringue use the whisk to whip the cream until stiff, then having carefully peeled off the bottom paper sandwich the two discs together with the cream and sliced or whole fruit. If you like you can also decorate the top with more fruit.

*Meringues can be flavoured in many different ways and this combination is both subtle and slightly unusual.*

Bring the vinegar to the boil, take it off the heat, stir in the instant coffee and leave it to cool completely before using.

Prepare two baking sheets by lining them with silicone paper or very well greased greaseproof paper and set the oven at Mark ¼, 200°F, 100°C.

Start by fitting the double-bladed knife and processing the demerara sugar for 10–20 seconds or until it has the consistency of caster sugar. Set the sugar on one side and wash the bowl and dry it. Fit the whisk and whisk the egg whites for 1½–2 minutes or until they are stiff but not dry. With the motor running add the caster sugar and continue whisking for a further 20–25 seconds or until it is smooth and shiny. Add the demerara sugar and the vinegar/coffee mixture and stop the whisk after 4–5 seconds or the moment the meringue as amalgamated. Spoon the meringues onto the prepared baking sheets and bake for 1½–2 hours or until they have dried out. Serve with whipped cream or ice cream or use the egg yolks to make the coffee butter icing given in the Genoese Sponge Cake recipe on page 75.

# Coffee and Brown Sugar Meringues

5 oz (150 g) demerara sugar
4 egg whites
2 oz (50 g) caster sugar
2 teaspoons white wine vinegar
1 teaspoon instant coffee

Makes 15–20 meringues

# Whisked Sponge

*A whisked fatless sponge should be so light that it will almost float on air. Maybe this one can't quite achieve that but the result is very impressive. You can, if you like, bake the cake in two sandwich tins, but I prefer to use one cake tin and then to cut the cold cake in half and sandwich it together with whipped cream and fruit or jam.*

*You can just dredge a little icing sugar over the finished cake or, during the strawberry season ice and decorate it as shown.*

4 eggs
4 oz (100 g) caster sugar
4 oz (100 g) plain flour
½ teaspoon baking powder

Set the oven to heat to Mark 4, 350°F, 175°C and grease and flour an 8″ (20 cm) cake tin.

Mix the flour and the baking powder, sift them and leave them on one side.

Fit the whisk, put the eggs and sugar into the Magimix and whisk them together for 4-5 minutes or until they are thick and fluffy. Remove the lid, sprinkle in the flour and whisk for 2 seconds. Stop and scrape down before whisking for a further 2 seconds. Turn the mixture into the prepared tin and bake it for 25 to 30 minutes or until the top is golden brown and springy to the touch. Leave the cake to cool in the tin for 3–4 minutes and then turn it out onto a wire cake rack. Remove the lining paper and leave it until it is completely cold.

**Icing**
8 oz (225 g) icing sugar
2 strawberries
Lemon juice

Put the icing sugar and strawberries into the Magimix and process for about 10 seconds then slowly drip in a little lemon juice. You need to add enough to achieve the right consistency.

The strawberries will have added both colour and moisture so you will only need a spoonful or so of lemon juice.

Using the Magimix Whisk to make a fatless sponge cake.

Making the icing and glazing the strawberries.

Put the sugar and water in a small saucepan and stir over a low heat until the sugar has melted. Turn up the heat and boil fast until you reach 'soft-ball' stage (240°F, 116°C on a sugar thermometer). Leave the syrup to cool a little then holding the strawberries by the stalk dip them in and lay them on a sheet of silicone or greaseproof paper to dry.

Spread the icing over the cake, using a spatula to smooth it down. Leave it to set a little before arranging the strawberries on the top.

**Decoration**
4 oz (100 g) granulated sugar
4 fl oz (120 ml) water
9 strawberries

73

## Genoese Sponge Cake with Coffee Icing

*A Genoese Cake keeps fresh for longer than a fatless sponge and is very suitable for icing. It is, in fact, the French equivalent of our Victoria Sponge and to quote Tante Marie: 'it is the basis of a great many delicious cakes and is a solid cake but very tender in texture'. The processing or pulsing in of the butter and flour must be done very quickly for if you overmix this cake it will separate. It is better to undermix the cake and then, using a spatula, to cut it through a few times in the cake tin to amalgamate the mixture. I have given a French coffee butter icing, but this is rich and for an 'occasion' and for everyday it can be sandwiched with jam and dusted with icing sugar.*

2 oz (50 g) butter
4 eggs
4 oz (100 g) caster sugar
4 oz (100 g) plain flour
½ teaspoon vanilla essence
(optional)

Set the oven to heat at Mark 4, 350°F, 175°C and grease and bottom line two 7″ (18 cm) sandwich tins.

Melt the butter and leave it on one side to cool, it wants to be nearly cold before you use it.

Fit the Magimix Whisk and whisk the eggs and sugar together for 4–5 minutes or until the mixture is very light yellow and fluffy. Stop scrape down and add about ⅔rds of the flour. Pulse it in by switching the machine on and off no more than three times.

Add the remaining flour, the butter and any flavouring and a pulse it in in the same way. Pour the mixture into the tins and bake it for 20–25 minutes or until it is golden brown on top and has shrunk from the sides of the tins.

Leave the cakes in the tins for a few minutes before turning them out onto a wire rack to cool.

Heat the water and sugar in a small saucepan and stir until the sugar has dissolved. Turn up the heat and bring the syrup to the boil and continue boiling for about 5 minutes or until 'soft ball' stage; 240°F, 116°C on a sugar thermometer.

Take the syrup off the heat and leave it to cool for a minute. Meanwhile fit the double-bladed knife and process to break up the egg yolks. With the machine running pour the syrup in a steady stream in through the feed tube. Leave the machine running add the butter in small cubes through the feed tube and finally the coffee. Continue processing for another 30 seconds or so or until the icing thickens up. If it is still too soft to use cool it in the fridge for a few minutes. Use some of the icing to sandwich the cakes together then keeping back 2 or 3 tablespoons to pipe on as decoration, spread the rest over the top and sides of the cake.

**Icing**
4 oz (100 g) granulated sugar
4 fl oz (120 ml) water
3 egg yolks
6 oz (175 g) butter, preferably unsalted
1 teaspoon instant coffee dissolved in 1 tablespoon boiling water

---

# American Brownies

*Another great American Cake that is always popular with all age groups. Brownies should be crisp on the outside and sticky on the inside and in the States are nearly always made with Baker's unsweetened chocolate. Bakers chocolate is very difficult to obtain over here but I find that the whisked method given here gives a very good result.*

Set the oven to Mark 3, 325°F, 160°C and grease and bottom line an 8″ (20 cm) square cake tin.

Process the walnuts for about 5 seconds or until roughly chopped and set them on one side.

Put the butter in a saucepan over a low heat and when it has melted stir in the vanilla essence and cocoa and leave it on one side.

Fit the Magimix whisk and whisk the eggs and sugar for 4-5 minutes or until they are light coloured and fluffy. Pour in the butter mixture whisk for a further 3–5 seconds to incorporate it and then transfer the mixture to a large bowl. Sprinkle over the flour and using a metal spoon fold it in and then very gently stir in the walnuts.

Turn the mixture into the prepared tin and bake for 45–50 minutes. On removal from the oven allow the Brownies to cool for about 10 minutes before cutting them into squares and putting them on a wire rack.

3 oz (75 g) walnuts
3 oz (75 g) butter
½ teaspoon vanilla essence
3 tablespoons cocoa
2 eggs
8 oz (225 g) caster sugar
3 oz (75 g) self raising flour

# Cherry and Praline Gâteau

**Praline**
3 oz (75 g) hazelnuts
4 oz (100 g) granulated sugar
3 fl oz (90 ml) water

*This cake has several different stages but it is not that complicated or difficult to make. If you prefer it the praline can be made in advance and, in fact, it will keep for some time in an airtight jar.*

Heat the oven to Mark 4, 350°F, 175°C. Spread the hazelnuts out onto a baking sheet and heat them in the oven for about 10 minutes. Watch them carefully for they burn easily and may need turning over after 5 minutes. Put the hot hazelnuts into a clean kitchen towel and rub it in your hands to flake off the skin.

Make a syrup by stirring the sugar and water together over a low heat and when the sugar has completely melted, turn the heat up to full. While it is boiling take a sheet of foil, oil or grease it well, and lay it out flat on a work surface. When the syrup starts to change colour, about 325°F, 162°C on a sugar thermometer, add the hazelnuts. Continue boiling for a minute or two more or until the mixture is a good caramel colour. On taking the saucepan off the heat immediately pour the mixture onto the foil and then leave it until it is cold and hard. Finally, break it up into lumps and process it for about 30 seconds or until powdered.

Making the Praline.

Finishing the cake.

## Cake
2 oz (50 g) hazelnuts
4 oz (100 g) caster sugar
4 eggs
2 oz (50 g) plain flour
1 teaspoon baking powder

Heat the oven to mark 5, 375°F, 190°C and grease and line a 10" (25 cm) cake tin.

Warm the nuts in the hot oven and rub them in a clean tea towel to de-skin them; process them for 35–40 seconds or until very finely ground, remove the nuts to a bowl and sift the flour and baking powder on top of them.

Fit the whisk and whisk the eggs and sugar together for 4-5 minutes or until the mixture is light yellow and fluffy. Add the nuts, flour and baking powder, whisk for 2 seconds, stop, scrape down and whisk for a further 2 seconds to just amalgamate the mixture.

Turn it into the prepared tin and bake it for 20 minutes or until the cake is shrinking from the sides of the tin. Leave the cake in the tin for a few minutes before turning it out onto a wire rack to cool.

## Filling
2 egg whites
10 fl oz (300 ml) double cream
3 tablespoons praline

Use the whisk to whisk the egg whites until stiff. Remove the egg whites and whisk the cream until thick. Return the stiff egg whites, add the praline and pulse the motor a few times to mix them in.

Cut the cold sponge in half and sandwich it together using about two-thirds of the filling.

## Topping and Decoration
1½ lbs (675 g) fresh cherries
3 tablespoons apricot jam
3 tablespoons redcurrant jelly
2 oz flaked almonds

Brown the almonds under the grill or by putting them in the oven for a few minutes.

Stone the cherries using a cherry stoner or the end of a potato peeler and place them decoratively on the cake. Warm the jam and jelly, stirring to mix them together, and glaze the cherries by brushing the jam mixture gently over them. Using a spatula or palette knife, spread the remaining filling round the sides of the cake and stud it with the flaked almonds.

*This is a fatless, whisked egg white, sandwich cake. I give a lemon curd filling but you could use jam and cream or a butter icing.*

Grease an 8″ (20 cm) cake tin and bottom line it with greased proof or silicone paper. Set the oven to heat at Mark 4, (350°F, 175°C).

Place the flour, cornflour, baking powder, lemon zest and half the sugar in the Magimix and process 7–10 seconds to mix and aerate them. Add the egg yolks and lemon juice and flick the pulse two or three times to just mix them in.

Using a clean Magimix bowl and the Whisk, beat the egg whites for about 1½ minutes until they are stiff and glossy. Do not overbeat or they will become dry and granular. Add the remaining sugar and whisk for a further 5 seconds.

Using a large bowl and a metal spoon, gently fold the two mixtures into each other, and then pour it all into the prepared tin.

Bake the cake for about 30 minutes or until it is golden brown and shrinking from the sides of the tin. Leave it to cool in the tin for about 5 minutes before turning it out onto a wire rack.

Put all the ingredients in a bowl set over a pan of hot water. Stir to melt the butter and sugar and then continue to cook the mixture, still stirring constantly, until it thickens enough to coat the back of a wooden spoon.

Leave the cake and the filling until they are both cold before cutting the cake into three layers and sandwiching it together with the lemon curd. Just before serving dust the top with icing sugar.

# Lemon Sponge

3 oz (75 g) self raising flour
1 oz (25 g) cornflour
1 teaspoon baking powder
Zest of a lemon
5 oz (150 g) icing sugar
2 tablespoons lemon juice
4 eggs separated

**Filling**
3 oz (75 g) caster sugar
Zest and juice of a large lemon
2 oz butter
1 egg and 1 egg yolk

79

# Strawberry Roulade

*I find this slightly unusual method and order of making a sponge cake works very well in a Magimix, but you must, as always, be extremely careful not to over-process the mixture and land up with something heavy and lead like.*

*Don't be frightened of rolling it up for if it does crack it doesn't really matter and you always disguise it by thickly dredging the roulade with more icing sugar.*

2 oz (50 g) almonds
5 oz (120 g) icing sugar
2 oz (50 g) self raising flour
½ teaspoon baking powder
Zest of an orange
5 eggs separated
Juice of ½ an orange

Set your oven to Mark 4, 350°F, 175°C. Grease a swiss roll tin of approximately 13″ × 9″ (33 cm × 23 cm) then line the bottom with a piece of greased greaseproof paper or silicone paper.

Put the almonds in the Magimix and process them for 45 seconds to a minute or until they are 'ground'. Place 3 oz of the sugar, the flour, baking powder and orange zest in the Magimix and process for 5 seconds to mix and sift them. Add the egg yolks and the orange juice and process until just mixed (about 3 seconds). Turn this mixture into a large bowl and carefully wash and dry the Magimix bowl.

Fit the Magimix Whisk and whisk the egg whites for 2 minutes or until they are stiff. Add the remaining sugar and whisk for a further 15–20 seconds. Using a metal spoon gently fold the meringue into the cake mixture and when it has amalgamated turn it into the tin. Smooth over the top and bake it for about 20–25 minutes or until it is springy and starts to shrink from the sides of the tin.

Cover it with a piece of greased paper and leave it until the roulade is completely cold. It will shrink slightly as it cools.

## Filling
10 fl oz (300 ml) double or
  whipping cream
8 oz (225 g) fresh strawberries or
½–¾ of a pot of good strawberry
  jam

I find that the easiest way to roll it up is to use a damp tea cloth which I lay flat on a work surface and sprinkle with icing sugar. Turn the roulade onto the tea towel, peel off the greased paper and being careful not to go too near the edges, spread it with the filling. Then, using the tea cloth, roll it up; do not do it too tightly or the filling will squash out. Roll it onto a plate and dredge it with more icing sugar.

Whilst the roulade is cooling, prepare the filling by whisking the cream until stiff and if using fresh strawberries cutting them into the cream and stirring them in. If you are using jam, it is better to spread it onto the roulade first before covering it with the cream. You can of course fill it with any fruit or jam and I have had a great success with very lightly cooked blackberries.

Making the Strawberry Roulade.    Filling and rolling the Chocolate Roulade.

*Roulades always seem to impress my guests, and this makes me feel that I am something of a cheat, for they are very easy and quick to make. This slightly unusual one, which uses breadcrumbs instead of flour, could certainly hold its own at any dinner party. Chocolate and bread are a good combination and this recipe seems to make a very moist and light cake. The filling made of grated chocolate and whipped cream is especially easy to make in the Magimix, but if you prefer it you could use cream on its own. (recipe overleaf)*

# Chocolate
# Roulade

1 oz (50 g) almonds or ground
   almonds
2 oz (50 g) bread (crusts
   removed)
½ teaspoon baking powder
1 oz (25 g) cocoa
5 oz (150 g) icing sugar
5 eggs, separated

Set the oven to Mark 4, 350°F, 175°C, grease a swiss roll tin of approximately 13 × 9″ (33 × 23 cm) and line the bottom with silicone or greased greaseproof paper.

If using whole almonds put them in the Magimix and process them for about 40–50 seconds or until they are very finely chopped and leave them in the bowl. If using ready ground almonds add them with the cocoa.

Put the bread into the Magimix and process for about 30 seconds or until you have fine breadcrumbs. Add the cocoa and half the sugar and process for 5 seconds to mix and aerate the dry ingredients, then add the egg yolks and process again, but very briefly, for about 3 seconds, to mix them in.

Using a clean Magimix bowl and the Whisk, whisk the egg whites for about 1½ minutes or until they are stiff, add the remaining sugar and beat for a further 5 seconds to incorporate it.

Using a metal spoon and a large bowl carefully fold the meringue mixture into the chocolate mixture and when it is amalgamated pour it into the prepared tin. Gently smooth over the top and bake it for 20–25 minutes or until the top is slightly springy to the touch.

Do not worry if the roulade, which will have risen enormously in the oven, shrinks as it cools, but leave it until it is completely cold before rolling it up.

**Filling**
10 fl oz (300 ml) double cream
4 oz (100 g) plain chocolate

Pour the cream into the Magimix bowl and use the whisk to whip it until it will just hold its shape. Change the whisk for the grating disc, grate the chocolate into the bowl and lightly stir it into the cream before filling the roulade. To roll it up follow the instructions for the Strawberry Roulade on page 80.

---

# Brown Bread Roulade

*The basic ingredients for this roulade are similar to those used for the Chocolate Roulade. However, the brown bread makes it unusual and it is versatile for it could, of course, be filled with a different jam or with fresh fruit and cream.*

Set the oven to Mark 4, 175°F, 350°C and line a 13 × 9″ (33 × 23 cm) swiss roll tin with silicone paper.

1 oz (25 g) almonds
2 oz (50 g) fresh brown bread
   (crusts removed)
1 oz (25 g) self raising flour
3 oz (75 g) icing sugar
5 eggs, separated
½ teaspoon vanilla essence

Process the almonds in the Magimix for about 10 seconds or until they are coarsely chopped, add the bread and process for about another 10 seconds or until you have fine breadcrumbs. Add the flour, half the sugar, the egg yolks and the vanilla essence and process no more than 3 or 4 seconds or until everything is just mixed. Transfer the mixture to a large bowl, fit the Magimix with a clean and dry bowl and the Whisk, and whisk the egg whites until they are stiff; this will take about 2 minutes.

Add the remaining sugar and whisk for another 20 seconds or until the meringue is smooth and glossy. Using a large metal spoon gently fold the meringue into the egg yolk mixture and then spoon it carefully into the prepared tin. Smooth over the top and bake it for 20 to 25 minutes or until it is golden brown and springy to the touch. Leave the roulade in the tin until it is completely cold then spread it with the apricot jam and, if liked, whipped cream and follow the instructions for the Strawberry Roulade to roll it up.

**Filling**
8 oz (225 g) apricot jam
5 fl oz (150 ml) double cream

---

# Vanilla Party Sponge

*This cake which has a good light texture is ideal for a birthday cake. It is very versatile and can be filled with any flavour you like and iced in any colour. I have given a plain vanilla cake with a vanilla icing; if you use proper vanilla essence which can be obtained from many health food shops you will find that the resulting cake is not at all dull but quite delicious. It can be decorated as you like or just left plain with the birthday candles on it. I have given instructions for baking it in two 7" (18 cm) tins, but if you want a bigger cake, make the recipe twice and bake each cake in a 9" (23 cm) sandwich tin.*

Set the oven to heat to Mark 4, 350°F, 175°C and grease and bottom line two 7" (18 cm) sandwich tins.

Melt the butter and set it on one side to cool. Sift the flour and cornflour together and leave them on one side.

Fit the Magimix Whisk and whisk the eggs and sugar together for 4-5 minutes or until the mixture is pale yellow and fluffy. Stop and spoon in about ⅔rds of the flour mixture and pulse it in by switching the machine on and off two or three times. Add the remaining flour, the cooled butter and the vanilla essence and pulse it in in the same way. Pour the mixture into the prepared tin and bake it for 20–25 minutes or until it is golden and springy to the touch. Leave the cake in the tin for a few minutes before turning it out onto a rack to cool.

1 oz (25 g) butter
3 oz (75 g) plain flour
1 oz (25 g) cornflour
4 eggs
4 oz (100 g) caster sugar
½ teaspoon vanilla essence

Put all the ingredients in the Magimix and process for about 10 seconds or until the butter cream is smooth. If you want a slightly lighter filling add a teaspoonful of very hot water and process it in. Sandwich the cakes together but try to keep them neat and tidy and flat on the top.

**Vanilla Butter Cream Filling**
2 oz (50 g) butter
4 oz (100 g) icing sugar
½ teaspoon vanilla essence

Put the sugar and a tablespoonful of water in the Magimix and process until smooth. Adjust the consistency to a heavy pouring one by adding either a few drops of water or another spoonful or so of sugar. Spoon the finished icing onto the cake and use a spatula to smooth it down. Decorate it as you wish.

**Glacé Icing**
6 oz (175 g) icing sugar
Water

Profiteroles with Chocolate
Ganache (*see p. 86*).

Choux Pastry mixture forming a
skin on the bottom of a saucepan
and ready for the Magimix.

The finished mixture after
processing.

# Choux Pastry

Choux pastry is marvellously easy to make in the Magimix and endlessly useful. I make it with strong plain flour, for the extra gluten means that the pastry puffs up more when cooking, but this is not essential and very satisfactory choux pastry can be made using ordinary plain flour.

I have given a selection of the more classic fillings and icings, but you can, of course, swop them round or use you imagination and let rip.

Try eclairs filled with strawberries crushed with cream and sugar and then decorated with syrup dipped strawberries as shown on page 72. Children love cream puffs filled with their favourite ice cream and for special celebration or Christmas party you could fill them with a mixture of sweetened chestnut purée and whipped cream.

I have given one savoury recipe, but here again there are many possibilities; little profiteroles can be served with drinks or eaten as a first course filled with chicken liver paté or with an avocado puréed in the Magimix with some mayonnaise and a few drops of Tabasco.

The basic recipe, given below, makes quite a lot of choux pastry: up to 30 eclairs, 50 profiteroles, 20 choux buns or a Gâteau St. Honoré and some little profiteroles. In the recipes I have given quantities for filling and icing half this amount, however it is very often worth while making the full amount for cooked choux pastry freezes well, and after de-frosting, the eclairs or buns just need five minutes in a hot oven to re-crisp them. If you do want to make a half quantity of the pastry I suggest that you replace the 3 (size 2) eggs with 2 (size 5) eggs.

Put the butter and water into a pan and heat it gently until the butter has melted. Turn up the heat and the moment the water boils take the pan off the heat and add the flour. Beat the mixture with a wooden spoon, return the pan to the heat and continue beating until a skin forms on the bottom of the pan. Put the mixture into the Magimix and leave it until it is cold, then start the motor and add the eggs, one at a time, through the feed tube. Stop the machine, scrape down and then process for a further 3–5 seconds until the pastry is mixed and looks glossy and yellow coloured. Use as required.

8 fl oz (240 ml) water
3 oz (75 g) butter
5 oz (150 g) strong plain flour
3 eggs

# Profiteroles

1 recipe choux pastry

**Filling**
½ pint (300 ml) double cream
1 desertspoon icing sugar
1 egg white (optional)

**Ganache Icing**
4 oz (100 g) plain chocolate
¼ pint (150 g) double cream

Set the oven to Mark 6, 400°F, 200°C.

Make the choux pastry and then using a wet spoon put it in small round mounds on a cold, damp baking sheet or one lined with silicone paper. You could pipe it if you prefer.

Bake the buns for about 20 minutes (the exact time depends on the size of the buns) or until they have at least doubled in size and are golden yellow. On removal from the oven prick each one with a skewer to allow the steam to escape and then transfer them to a wire rack to cool.

Whip the cream until stiff and then stir in the icing sugar. If you want a lighter filling fold a stiffly beaten egg white into the cream and sugar mixture.

Slit round a third to half the bottom of each profiterole with a sharp knife and then use a teaspoon to fill each one.

Melt the chocolate in a small bowl standing over a saucepan of very hot water. Leave the chocolate to cool slightly then stir in the cream.

Pile the profiteroles into a pyramid on a large plate, you will need three or four for each person, and carefully pour over the chocolate ganache.

---

# Savoury Profiteroles

1 recipe choux pastry
1 oz (50 g) grated Parmesan cheese
½ teaspoon of salt
¼ teaspoon cayenne pepper

**Filling**
4 oz (100 g) cream cheese
5 fl oz (150 ml) thick plain yoghurt
1 tin, 1.75 oz (50 g) anchovy fillets
freshly ground black pepper

*Very more-ish and ideal for a drinks party. You can always fill left over or frozen profiteroles with a savoury mixture, but they are just that much better if the cheese and seasonings are added to the basic choux pastry. They are also better if served warm and only filled at the last minute.*

Follow the instructions on page 85 for making the choux pastry and add the cheese, salt and cayenne pepper with the eggs and process them into the mixture.

Set the oven to Mark 6, 200°C, 400°F, and using a wet teaspoon drop little mounts of the pastry onto a cold, damp baking sheet, or one lined with silicone paper. Bake the profiteroles for 20 minutes or until they have puffed up and are golden coloured.

On removal from the oven prick each one with a skewer and then transfer them to a wire rack to cool.

Put the cheese, yoghurt, drained and roughly cut up anchovy fillets and a good sprinkling of pepper into the Magimix and process until you have a smooth mixture. Refrigerate the mixture, to stiffen it up, for at least half an hour before using it.

Just before serving re-warm the savoury profiteroles in the oven then cut them open and use a teaspoon to fill each one with the cream cheese and anchovy mixture.

Savoury Profiteroles.

# Gâteau St Honoré

*France still remains very regional in its food, tastes and specialities and the Gâteau St. Honoré, which incidentally is named after the patron saint of pastry cooks, is one of the great Parisien desserts. Many pâttisièrs in Paris open on Sunday mornings and they nearly all have the most beautiful and mouth-watering Gâteau St. Honoré in the centre of the window.*

*A really genuine Gâteau St. Honoré is made by baking a circle of choux pastry onto a round disc of pâte sucrée and then filling the choux pastry with cream and the middle with crème pâttisière. This is, however, very rich and perhaps overdone for todays taste, so it is made with just a circle of cream filled choux pastry, topped with little balls or profiteroles, glazed with caramel and decorated with cream and crystallized violets. The crystallized violets are totally authentic, very pretty and much nicer than the glacé cherries that I have seen suggested in some English recipes.*

1 recipe choux pastry
10 fl oz (300 ml) double cream
2 tablespoons icing sugar
6 oz (175 g) granulated sugar
5 fl oz (150 ml) water
crystallised violets to decorate

Make the choux pastry following the instruction on page 85. Line two baking sheets with silicone paper and draw an 8″ (20 cm) circle onto one of them. Set the oven to heat to Mark 6, 400°F, 200°C.

Fit a ½″ (1.25 cm) nozzle to a piping bag and following the drawn circle carefully pipe a generous circle onto the tray. Change to a smaller nozzle (you can use a star) and pipe a dozen or so little buns onto the other baking tray. Try to make them the same size, round and not to ragged at the edges. You will probably have some pastry over and you can make more little profiteroles or use it for eclairs or cream puffs. Bake them following the instructions for the cream puffs on page 91.

You can make the choux pastry ahead, but when you are ready to assemble the cake have everything by you, for the use of caramel means that you have to work reasonably quickly.

Whip the cream until stiff and stir in the icing sugar. Put the sugar and water into a saucepan, place it over a low heat and stir

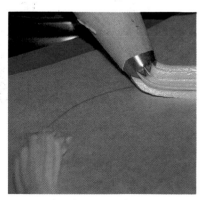

Piping the choux circle.

Spooning the little balls onto a baking sheet.

Sticking the little profiteroles onto the Gâteau.

frequently until the sugar has completely dissolved. Stop stirring, turn the heat right up and let it boil fast until it is just turning colour (about 325°F, 170°C on a sugar thermometer). You want to have a light rather than a dark coloured caramel. The moment it has reached the right colour pour in a tablespoonful of water (be careful for it will spit). Swirl it round the saucepan until it is all amalgamated and then keep the saucepan over a low heat while you assemble the cake.

Cut round the outside perimeter at the bottom of the circle and using a piping bag fill the circle with cream, then place it in position on a plate. Cut out the centre of 10 of the little profiterolles and fill each one with cream.

Use a pastry brush and brush the whole of the top of the circle with caramel, then blobbing on a little more, so that they stick on, position the buns evenly round the top. Leave them for a minute or so, for the caramel to cool and for them to stick in position, then brush generously over the top of each one with the caramel mixture. Finally pipe a blob of cream between each little bun and top it with a piece of crystallised violet.

The finished Gâteau St. Honoré will keep for several hours in a cool place.

# Eclairs with Chocolate or Coffee Glacé Icing

½ recipe choux pastry

**Filling**
½ pint (300 ml) double cream
1 egg white

**Glacé Icing**
4 oz (100 g) icing sugar
1 desertspoon cocoa powder or
   instant coffee powder
1 tablespoon hot water

Make the choux pastry as given in the recipe on page 85. Preheat the oven to Mark 6, 200°F, 400°C. Use a piping bag fitted with a plain ½″ (1.25 cm) nozzle and pipe the eclairs onto a cold and damp baking sheet or one covered with silicone paper, cutting each one off neatly at the end using a wet knife. You will probably finish up with about 25–30 eclairs. Bake them for 20 to 25 minutes, or until they have puffed up and are golden in colour. When you remove them from the oven prick each one with a skewer to allow the steam to escape, and leave them on a wire rack until they are cold.

To fill: Whip the egg white until stiff: You can, of course, use the Magimix Whisk; and then separately whip the cream until stiff. Add the egg white to the cream and fold it in using a metal spoon. Either fill the eclairs from one end using a piping bag or slit them down the side and fill them with a spoon.

Stir the cocoa or coffee powder into the hot water and when it has melted add it to the icing sugar in the Magimix. Process for about 5 seconds until you have a smooth mixture. If the texture needs adjusting add a few drops more of water or a spoonful or so of icing sugar. Using a teaspoon dribble a little of the icing along the top of each eclair.

Make the choux pastry and then set the oven to Mark 6, 400°F, 200°C. Using a wet desertspoon spoon 15–20 balls of the pastry onto cold, damp baking sheets or ones spread with silicone paper. Bake the buns for 20 minutes and then turn the oven down to Mark 4, 350°F, 175°C and leave them for a further 5–10 minutes to dry out. On removal from the oven prick each one with a skewer and transfer them to a wire rack to cool.

Put the milk into a saucepan and set it over a gentle heat. Process the egg yolks, cornflour and sugar for about 5 seconds, then, with the motor working, pour the hot milk in through the feed tube. Pour the custard mixture back into the saucepan, return it to the heat and stir constantly until the mixture thickens, then leave it on one side until cold. Using a sharp knife cut round the bottoms of the cream puffs and fill each one with a spoonful of Crème Pâtissière.

Use a strainer to dust icing sugar over each bun, and using either a teaspoon or a piping bag with a thin nozzle dribble a little melted chocolate over the top.

# Cream Puffs with Crème Pâtissière Filling

1 recipe choux pastry

**Crème Pâtissière**
10 fl oz (300 ml) milk
2 egg yolks
1 tablespoon cornflour
3 oz (75 g) caster sugar
½ teaspoon vanilla essence

**Icing**
Icing sugar
2 oz (50 g) plain chocolate

# Biscuits

## Brandy Snaps

*Crispy brandy snaps filled with whipped cream are a lovely treat and as they can be cooked ahead and kept in a tin they make a useful and easy to assemble dessert. I always had trouble rolling them until I discovered the secret of baking them on squares of Bakewell paper and then turning them to cool slightly onto a larger sheet. This completely eliminates the problem of them dripping over the side of a spatula and breaking, and makes the rolling quick and almost foolproof. I do, however, find that the handle of a wooden spoon is not really quite big enough and one needs a piece of dowelling of about ³⁄₄″ (2 cm) diameter, which is easily obtainable from any builders merchants – or failing that a small broom handle will do.*

5 oz (150 g) golden syrup
3 oz (75 g) soft light brown sugar
4 oz (100 g) butter
1 teaspoon lemon juice
4 oz (100 g) plain flour
1 teaspoon ground ginger

Makes 30–35 biscuits

Heat the oven to Mark 5, 375°F, 190°C. If you have room for three layers of baking trays cut out six squares of Bakewell paper of about 6″ × 6″ (18 cm square) and two extra sheets which are slightly larger. Place two of the squares on each baking sheet.

Put the syrup, sugar, butter and lemon juice into a pan and leave over a low heat, stirring occasionally until the sugar has melted. Put the flour and ginger into the Magimix and then, with the motor working, pour the syrup and butter mixture in through the feed tube. Process for 5 seconds, or until mixed.

Drop a spoonful of the mixture into the centre of each square of paper and then flatten it out slightly. Put the trays in the oven at about three minute intervals and as they take about 8 minutes to cook this means that you should be able to keep a production line going.

(recipe continued overleaf)

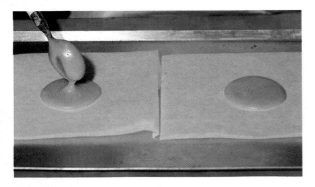

Roll the brandy snaps before they cool and harden.

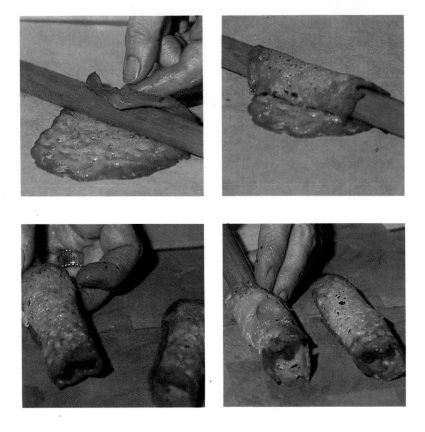

After about 8 minutes the biscuits should have spread out, be dark brown round the edges and bubbling all over. Remove them from the oven and using your hands pick up the squares of paper and turn the biscuits over onto the two larger sheets. Leave them to cool for a minute and while they are doing this put two more dollops of the mixture onto the paper and into the oven. Then lifting up the corner of the paper roll the biscuits over the stick and press the two ends together – you will probably be able to fit two biscuits onto the stick at the same time. Leave them to cool and harden for a couple of minutes while you take the next lot out of the oven, then slide the biscuits off the stick onto a wire tray and roll up the next two. Once you get the hang of it it really is very easy and a thoroughly satisfying thing to do.

The brandy snaps will keep well in an air-tight tin. Before serving fill them at both ends with whipped cream.

Set the oven to Mark 5, 375°F, 190°C, grease two baking sheets and if possible line them with silicone paper.

Melt the butter in a saucer placed over a saucepan of boiling water. You need to melt it slowly so that when you pour it into the Magimix it is liquid but not hot.

Put all the other ingredients into the bowl, pour over the butter and process for 3 seconds. Stop the machine and scrape down the bowl before processing for a further 2 seconds or until the mixture has amalgamated.

You can now use a teaspoon to place the mixture in blobs onto the prepared trays or you can pipe it on so that you get the traditionally shaped 'cats tongues'. You will find that the mixture is liquid for piping but the white of egg holds it together so it should be possible. Space the biscuits out well for they will spread in the oven. Bake them for about 12 minutes or until they are brown round the edge but still cream coloured in the centre. Use a spatula to remove them to a rack to cool and harden.

## Langues de Chat

3 oz (75 g) butter
3 oz (75 g) icing sugar
3 oz (75 g) plain flour
2 egg whites
½ teaspoon vanilla essence

Makes about 35–40 biscuits

# Chocolate Iced Almond Biscuits

2 oz (50 g) blanched almonds
4 oz (100 g) soft butter
4 oz (100 g) plain flour
2 oz (50 g) caster sugar
½ teaspoon vanilla essence
4 oz (100 g) plain chocolate

Makes 30–35 biscuits

*The almonds in these biscuits are processed until they are very finely chopped, but not to a paste, so that they still have some crunch left. The biscuits eaten on their own are good, but the chocolate is an excellent addition. The biscuit dough is very soft and you might find it easier to roll it out half at a time.*

Put the almonds in the Magimix and process them until they are very finely chopped (15–20 seconds). Add the butter, flour, sugar and vanilla essence and process until the mixture clings together, this will probably take no more than 5 to 7 seconds. Turn the dough out onto a floured board, you will find that it is very soft, form it into a ball and wrap it in cling film. Refrigerate it for at least half an hour, by which time the dough will have firmed up and be easier to roll out.

Set the oven to Mark 4, 350°F, 175°C, and grease two baking sheets. Roll the dough out until it is about ¼″ (.75 cm) thick and cut out the biscuits using a cutter of about 2″ (5 cm) in diameter. Place them on the baking sheets and bake for 8–10 minutes or until the edges just start to brown. When they are cooked use a spatula to move them to a wire rack to cool.

Wait until they are completely cold before you coat them with chocolate. Melt the chocolate in a saucer or small bowl over a saucepan of boiling water and using a teaspoon drop some into the centre of each biscuit and smooth it round. Leave them for the chocolate to harden which will take about half an hour.

Alternatively, and something that looks pretty, you could dip half of each biscuit in the chocolate.

# Delices d'Orange

8 oz (225 g) self raising flour
2 oz (50 g) icing sugar
5 oz (150 g) soft butter
  (preferably unsalted)
Grated zest of one large orange
2 tablespoons squeezed orange
  juice

*These biscuits are a family favourite and really are as light as a feather. They are equally suitable for a small's birthday party or for eating with strawberry ice-cream at a very grown-up dinner party.*

Heat your oven to Mark 5, 375°F, 190°C.

Grate the zest from the orange, then squeeze out the juice.

Place the flour and icing sugar in the bowl and process for 5 seconds to both aerate and mix them. Add the butter cut into lumps, together with the orange zest and juice. Process for 10 seconds.

Turn the mixture onto a floured surface and knead for a few seconds until it has amalgamated. Roll it into a ball with your hands before rolling it out, sprinkling with flour as necessary, until it is no more than ¼″ (.75 cm) thick. Use a pastry cutter to cut into rounds of about 2″ (5 cm) diameter, re-rolling when necessary. Bake the biscuits on a greased tray for about 8–10 minutes or until lightly golden. Transfer them to a wire tray to cool and wait until the biscuits are completely cold before icing them.

Place icing sugar and orange juice in the bowl and process for 5 seconds or until mixed but of a fairly stiff consistency. If it seems to be too thick add a few more drops of orange juice, or if too thin another spoonful of icing sugar and process briefly again. With a teaspoon dribble a little icing into the centre of each biscuit.

These biscuits will keep well in a tin, but once iced they need eating.

## Icing

2 tablespoons squeezed orange juice
5 oz (150 g) icing sugar

Chocolate Iced Almond Biscuits and Délices d'Orange.

The Almonds being ground for
Refrigerator Biscuits.

Ingredients for the Chocolate
Refrigerator Biscuits.

*Refrigerator biscuits are American by origin, are very easy to make and endlessly useful. The roll of dough can be kept in the refrigerator for up to two weeks, and biscuits are then shaved off as and when they are needed. Each of these 'rolls' will produce about 50 biscuits.*

Put all the ingredients into the Magimix and process them until they cling together and form a 'dough' ball (about 20–30 seconds). Turn the mixture on to a work surface and mould it into a roll of about 2″ (5 cm) diameter. Wrap it in foil or cling film and refrigerate it for several hours, until hard, or until needed.

To bake the biscuits shave them very thinly from the roll and bake on a greased baking sheet at Mark 5, 375°F, 190°C for 8–10 minutes or until the edges start to brown. On removal from the oven immediately loosen them with a spatula and then transfer them to a rack to cool.

# Chocolate Refrigerator Biscuits

7 oz (200 g) self raising flour
1 oz (25 g) cocoa powder
5 oz (150 g) caster sugar
4 oz (100 g) butter
1 egg

---

Put the almonds in the bowl and process them for 15–20 seconds until they are very finely chopped. Add the rest of the ingredients and process for about 10–20 seconds and until the mixture clings together and starts to form a 'dough' ball.

Turn the mixture out and using your hands mould it into a roll of about 2″ (5 cm) diameter. Wrap the roll in cling film and refrigerate it for several hours or until hard.

To bake the biscuits heat the oven to Mark 5, 375°F, 190°C, and then using a very sharp knife cut the thinnest biscuits possible off from the roll. Place these biscuits onto a greased baking sheet and bake for 8–10 minutes or until they start to brown. While still hot remove them to a rack to cool.

Serve them with ice cream or other desserts.

# Almond Refrigerator Biscuits

2 oz (50 g) almonds
6 oz (175 g) self-raising flour
5 oz (150 g) caster sugar
4 oz (100 g) soft butter
1 egg
A few drops almond essence
  (optional)

Cutting the biscuits.

# Chocolate Chip Cookies

*These biscuits are very more-ish and teenagers in particular seem to have an insatiable appetite for them. You can make them with plain flour but I rather like the mixture given in the recipe. They are also good if you add a few more nuts, of any variety, and leave out the chocolate.*

2 oz (50 g) walnuts
3 oz (75 g) self raising flour
2 oz (50 g) wholemeal flour
2 oz (50 g) light soft brown sugar
2 oz (50 g) caster sugar
3 oz (75 g) soft butter
1 egg
A few drops of vanilla essence (optional)
3 oz (75 g) chocolate chips

Makes 30–35 biscuits

Set the oven at Mark 5, 375°F, 190°C and well grease a couple of baking sheets.

Place the walnuts in the Magimix and pulse a few times to roughly chop them, then remove them and keep them on one side.

Put the flours, sugars, butter, egg and, if used, the vanilla essence into the bowl and process them for 7 seconds. Stop, scrape down, add the walnuts and chocolate chips and pulse three or four times to just mix them in.

Use a spoon to drop little mounds of the mixture onto the baking sheets – keep them well spaced out for they will spread in the oven. Bake the biscuits for 10–15 minutes or until they start to turn golden. On removal from the oven immediately (or they will harden and stick) lift the biscuits off the trays and put them to cool on a wire rack.

Spiced Cookies and Chocolate Chip Cookies.

# Spiced Cookies

5 oz (150 g) self raising flour
2 oz (50 g) soft light brown sugar
2 oz (50 g) granulated sugar
1 teaspoon mixed spice
½ teaspoon ground ginger
½ teaspoon ground mace
4 oz (100 g) soft butter
1 egg

Heat the oven to Mark 5, 375°F, 190°C and well grease two baking sheets.

Process the flour, sugars and spices together for a few seconds. Add the egg and the butter cut into lumps and process for 5 seconds. Stop and scrape down and process for a further 5 seconds or until the mixture draws together.

Use a teaspoon and drop them in dollops onto the baking sheets – they will spread in the oven so leave lots of room. Bake for 10–15 minutes or until the cookies are a light golden brown. Lift them off the baking sheets with a spatula and put them on a wire rack to harden.

*Very traditional but none the worse for that. The dough can be baked in rectangles, circles and then cut into petticoat tails, or pressed into one of those lovely hand carved traditional moulds that you can now buy in some specialist kitchen shops.*

Heat the oven to Mark 2, 300°F, 150°C.

Put all the ingredients into the Magimix and process them until the mixture turns into a dough ball.

Turn the dough out onto a work surface that has been dusted with flour and using a well floured pin roll it out. The dough will be very soft and you may find it easier to press it with your fingers into a well greased and floured swiss roll tin of approximately 7 × 10″ (18 × 25 cms). Prick all over the surface with a fork and bake for 30–35 minutes or until golden. On removal from the oven mark the surface into ractangles.

If you wish to make petticoat tails carefully roll the dough into two circles of about 8″ (20 cm) in diameter (use a plate to guide you) and then very gently transfer the circles to a greased baking sheet. Prick all over the top and crimp up the edges with your fingers. Bake until golden and mark into segments on removal from the oven. Leave to cool on the baking sheet.

# Shortbread

7 oz (200 g) plain flour
2 oz (50 g) cornflour
4 oz (100 g) caster sugar
6 oz (175 g) soft butter
A few drops of vanilla essence

Crimping the edge of the Petticoat Tails.

# Grasmere Shortcake

*In Grasmere, I believe, you can still find a shop that bakes and sells its own traditional shortcake and this one eaten on its own is certainly very good. With the icing, which the uncomparable Jane Grigson recommends, and which was added at Easter, it becomes rich but quite delicious.*

8 oz (225 g) plain flour
4 oz (100 g) soft dark brown
  sugar
1 teaspoon ground ginger
4 oz (100 g) butter
3 tablespoons milk

Pre-heat the oven to Mark 4, 350°F, 175°C, and grease and bottom line two 8″ (20 cm) sandwich tins.

Put the flour, sugar and ginger into the bowl and process them for about 5 seconds to mix them and, if necessary, de-lump the sugar. Add the butter (which should be hard) cut into cubes and process for 5–10 seconds or until you have reached the coarse breadcrumb stage. With the machine running add the milk through the feed tube and continue processing for a further 5 seconds. The mixture should have clung together, but will be fairly dry and crumbly.

Gently press the mixture into the tins and bake for 20 minutes or until the shortcake starts to colour. On removal from the oven immediately mark out the slices by cutting half way through the shortcake and then leave them in the tins until they are cold.

**French Butter Cream Filling**
3 pieces of stem ginger
3 oz (75 g) sugar
3 fl oz (90 ml) water
2 egg yolks
4 oz (100 g) unsalted butter
1 teaspoon syrup from the ginger
½ teaspoon ground ginger

Process the stem ginger until fairly finely chopped, remove and reserve. Put the sugar and water in a saucepan and stir over a low heat until the sugar has completely dissolved. Turn up the heat and boil until the soft ball stage is reached, (240°F, 116°C) this will take about five minutes. Place the egg yolks in the Magimix, start the motor and pour the hot syrup in through the feed tube followed by cubes of the butter. Leave the icing until it is cold; you can speed this up by putting it into the fridge; then add the ground ginger, the stem ginger and the syrup and process again

to thicken the mixture. You will find that it quickly resembles the consistency of whipped cream. Use the icing to sandwich the discs of shortcake together but do not do this more than an hour before serving it or the shortcake will go soggy. Finally dust the top with icing sugar.

Pouring the caramel and then the chocolate onto the Millionaire's Shortbread.

*This sweet gooey caramel and chocolate covered shortbread is loved by the grown-ups when the children aren't looking and loved by the children when the grown-ups aren't looking!*

Heat the oven to Mark 4, 350°F, 175°C and grease a 7 × 10″ (18 × 25 cm) tin. Put the flour, sugar and butter into the Magimix and process for 5–7 seconds using the pulse or 'on-off' method by which time the mixture will have started to amalgamate. Turn it into the prepared tin and using your fingers press it level, then bake for about 20 minutes or until it starts to colour. Remove the shortbread from the oven and leave it to cool slightly before pouring on the caramel filling.

Put all the ingredients into a saucepan, heat gently, stirring all the time until they are melted. Turn up the heat, bring the mixture to the boil, and still stirring, boil for from 5 to 8 minutes or until it is brown and caramel coloured. Leave it to cool for a few minutes and then pour it over the shortbread.

Break the chocolate into squares and put them in a saucer or small bowl over a saucepan of boiling water. Leave until it is completely melted and then pour it over the cold caramel. Use a fork to make a swirled pattern on the top and a sharp knife to cut it into squares.

# Millionaire's Shortbread

### Shortbread
5 oz (150 g) self raising flour
2 oz (50 g) caster sugar
4 oz (100 g) soft butter

### Caramel Filling
4 oz (100 g) butter
1 small can – 6 oz (193 g)
  condensed milk
3 oz (75 g) caster sugar
2 tablespoons golden syrup

### Chocolate Topping
7 oz (200 g) bar plain chocolate

Makes approximately 16 squares

103

# Gingerbread Men

*Making gingerbread men is a good ploy for a rainy afternoon. Children seem to love being let loose with the dough, a gingerbread man shaped cutter and a few raisins, and funnily enough this dough seems to be good tempered enough to survive it.*

2 oz (50 g) butter
2 heaped tablespoons golden
   syrup
3 oz (75 g) soft dark brown sugar
8 oz (225 g) self raising flour
1 teaspoon ground ginger
1 teaspoon cinnamon
A pinch of ground cloves
A few currants and/or glacé icing
   for decoration (optional)

Preheat the oven to Mark 4, 350°F, 175°C and grease two baking sheets. Put the butter, golden syrup and sugar in a small saucepan, set it over a low heat and stirring occasionally heat it until the contents melt, but do not let it come to the boil.

Put the flour and spices into the Magimix turn on the motor and then pour the syrup mixture in through the feed tube. Process for a further 5 seconds, then turn it out and knead it lightly until it is smooth and clings together. Wrap it in clingfilm and refrigerate it for 15–20 minutes before rolling it out.

Roll it out on a floured work surface to about ⅛ (5 mm) and cut out the men. Lay them on the baking sheets and decorate with a few currants for eyes, noses and buttons if you wish. Bake them for 12–15 minutes or until golden brown. Leave them to cool for a few minutes before transferring them to a wire rack.

For a party you can ice in eyes, noses, buttons and names using a little glacé icing and a thin nozzle.

*Children love making this and love eating the result. The only problem is that it should be left for up to twenty-four hours to harden before it is cut, however, this can be overcome by placing it in the freezer for an hour or so.*

# Uncooked Chocolate Biscuit Cake

Put the butter and golden syrup in a pan to melt. Meanwhile put the cocoa in the Magimix, sprinkle over the hot water and process to melt the cocoa. Add the butter and syrup together with the sugar and process for a few seconds to mix. Then add the biscuits which have been broken into pieces, and process using the pulse a few times until they are mixed in, but not totally cut into crumbs. Add the chocolate chips, the raisins and the walnuts, if used, and use the pulse two or three times to incorporate them into the mixture.

Turn the mixture out into a greased and bottom lined 8″ (20 cm) flan tin and press it in evenly. Either refrigerate it overnight before cutting or put it in the deep freeze for an hour or so to harden up.

To serve the cake turn it out onto a plate, lightly dust the top with a little icing sugar and perhaps sprinkle a few silver balls over the surface.

4 oz (100 g) butter
2 tablespoons golden syrup
2 oz (50 g) cocoa
4 tablespoons hot water
1 oz (25 g) caster sugar
8 oz (225 g) biscuits: Osborne, Marie or Digestive
2 oz (50 g) chocolate chips
1 oz (25 g) raisins
2 oz (50 g) walnuts (optional)

# Digestive Biscuits

*The texture of these biscuits is crunchy but rather coarser than bought digestive biscuits. This recipe is intended for sweet biscuits, but if you cut the amount of sugar down by at least half you will find that they make a good cheese biscuit.*

4 oz (100 g) wholewheat flour
2 oz (50 g) porridge oats
1 oz (25 g) light soft brown sugar
1 teaspoon baking powder
1/4 teaspoon salt
2 oz (50 g) butter
1 oz (25 g) lard
2 tablespoons milk

Makes 16–20 biscuits

Set the oven at Mark 4, 350°F, 175°C, and grease two baking sheets.

Put all the dry ingredients into the Magimix and pulse it several times to mix them together. Add the butter and lard and process until you reach the breadcrumb stage, (about 5 seconds), then with the motor running add the milk through the feed tube. Continue processing for another 15–20 seconds or until the mixture draws together.

Turn the mixture onto a floured work surface, form it into a ball and then roll it out until it is about 1/4″ (.75 cm) thick. Use a biscuit cutter of about 2½″ (7 cm) diameter to cut the dough into rounds. Prick all over the tops with a fork and bake the biscuits for 10–15 minutes or until the edges are slightly browned. Leave them to cool on the baking sheets.

---

# Oatcakes

*These being unsweetened are good with cheese and especially good with a hard mature Cheddar. However, I would also recommend trying them with butter and honey for breakfast.*

6 oz (175 g) medium oatmeal
2 oz (50 g) plain flour
1/4 teaspoon bicarbonate of soda
1/2 teaspoon salt
2 oz (50 g) lard
2 tablespoons boiling water

Makes about 20 biscuits

Grease one large or two small baking trays and set the oven to Mark 3, 325°F, 160°C.

Put the dry ingredients into the Magimix and process them for about 5 seconds to mix them. Add the lard, cut into lumps, and process for a further 5 seconds, then, with the machine running, add the boiling water through the feed tube. You will find that the mixture will cling together almost immediately. Turn it out onto a board that has been sprinkled with a mixture of flour and oatmeal and carefully, without too much pressure, or the dough will crack, roll it out to about 1/4″ (.75 cm) thickness. Cut out the biscuits using a 2½″ (7 cm) fluted cutter, gathering up the dough and re-rolling as necessary. Place them on the baking trays and bake them for about 20 minutes or until the edges start to brown. Use a spatula to remove them to a wire rack and when they are completely cold store them in an airtight container.

Oatcakes and Digestive Biscuits.
Rolling out the Oatcakes.

# Cheese Straws

2 oz (50 g) strong cheddar cheese
4 oz (100 g) plain flour
2 oz (50 g) soft butter
1 egg yolk
½ teaspoon salt
½ teaspoon mustard powder
   (optional)
pinch cayenne (optional)

*The ever popular cheese straws – and they are so easy to make in the Magimix.*

Grate the cheese using the standard grating disc, then leaving the cheese in the bowl change to the double-bladed knife. Add the remaining ingredients and process until the mixture clings together. If it does not amalgamate after about 20 seconds stop the motor and sprinkle in a few drops of cold water, then continue processing until the mixture clings together. Turn it out onto a floured work surface, form it into a ball, wrap it in cling-film and refrigerate it for about an hour.

Set the oven at Mark 6, 400°F, 200°C and grease two baking sheets. Roll the dough out until it is quite thin – about ⅛″ (.5 cm) and carefully cut the straws to about ¼″ (.75 cm) wide and 2″ (5 cm) long. Place them on the baking sheets and bake for 5–7 minutes or until they start to change colour. Remove them to a rack and let them cool slightly before eating them. You can, if you wish, store them in an airtight tin, but they are then nicer if you re-heat them before eating them.

If you want to serve them in 'bundles' just cut out a few extra long straws and turn them into circles on the baking tray.

*Beaten biscuits come from the Southern States of America and initially were tough to make for they were pounded or beaten by hand for up to three quarters of an hour. However, they can now be made very satisfactorily and in two minutes in a Magimix. The finished biscuits are plain and hard and are good eaten with cheese or any savoury spread.*

# Beaten Biscuits

Set the oven to Gas 4, 175°C, 350°F.

Put the flour, butter, cut into lumps, and the salt into the Magimix and process them for about 7 seconds or until the mixture reaches the breadcrumb stage. Keep the motor running and add the water through the feed tube. After a few seconds a pastry type ball will form round the double-bladed knife and once this happens continue processing or 'beating' the biscuits for another two minutes.

Flour your hands well, remove the dough from the bowl and then form it into a sausage shape. Roll the dough out until you have a rectangle which is about ⅛″ (.5 cm) thick. Fold one half of the rectangle over to make two layers and cut through them both using a round 2″ (5 cm) cutter. Re-roll and repeat as necessary.

Put the double-layered biscuits on an ungreased baking sheet, prick them with a fork and bake them for 25–30 minutes or until light golden coloured. Split the biscuits in half and return them to the oven, centre side down, for a further five minutes.

8 oz (225 g) plain flour
4 oz (100 g) hard butter
½ teaspoon salt
2½ tablespoons iced water

Makes approximately 18
    biscuits or 36 when split

109

# Parmesan and Anchovy Thins

*These little cheesy biscuits topped with anchovy are, I find, extremely popular and surprisingly enough even liked by children. They also make a very good ending to a dinner party. If possible do try to use fresh Parmesan, for it really is so much better than the ready grated bought variety.*

2 oz (50 g) Parmesan cheese
4 oz (100 g) plain flour
2 oz (50 g) soft butter
1 egg yolk
1 tin 1.75 oz (50 g) anchovy fillets
1 tablespoon olive oil

Makes 35–40 biscuits

Use the parmesan disc and grate the cheese. Leave the parmesan in the bowl, but remove the disc and fit the double-bladed knife. Add the flour, butter and egg yolk and process until the mixture amalgamates and draws together. If it does not do this in 20 seconds stop the motor, sprinkle in a few drops of cold water and process for a further 5–10 seconds. Turn the biscuit dough out onto a floured surface and shape it into a ball. Wrap it in cling-film and refrigerate it for about an hour before rolling it out.

Set the oven to heat at Mark 6, 400°F, 200°C and well grease two baking sheets. Empty the tin of anchovies into the Magimix (which need not have been washed), add the oil and process until you have a paste, about 30 seconds.

Roll the dough out very thinly and cut it into rounds using a cutter of approximately 2″ (5 cm) diameter. Place the biscuits on the baking sheets and, using a pastry brush or small spatula, spread each one with the anchovy paste. Bake the biscuits for 8–10 minutes or until they are golden round the edge.

Serve them while they are hot or remove them to a wire rack to cool. They can be heated up again if you wish.

# Gruyère and Bacon Slices

*These cheese and bacon slices are delicious for nibbling, and as they can be eaten in the fingers they are easy to serve as a savoury after dinner or you could leave them uncut, wrap them in foil and take them on a picnic.*

2 oz (50 g) Gruyère cheese
3 oz (75 g) plain flour
2 oz (50 g) soft butter
Yolk of an egg
Pinch salt
Freshly ground black pepper
½ teaspoon mustard powder
A little cold water
4 rashers thin cut streaky bacon
Canadian style or similar

Makes 24 slices

Grate the cheese into the bowl and then change to the double-bladed knife. Add the flour, butter, egg, seasonings (if the bacon is very salty you may need to omit the salt) and about half a teaspoonful of cold water. Process them for about 5 seconds, by which time the ingredients should have amalgamated. You do not want too dry a dough for this recipe or it will be very fiddly when you roll it out. Turn it onto a floured work surface, mould it into a smooth ball, wrap it in cling film and put it in the fridge for about half an hour.

While it is resting gently fry the bacon rashers for a few minutes to release the fat, but do not let them brown. Drain them on kitchen paper.

Turn the oven on to heat up to Mark 3, 325°F, 160°C and grease a baking sheet.

Turn the cheese dough back onto the floured board and carefully roll it out – you want to roll it into four rectangles of approximately 3 × 5″ (7.5 × 12.5 cm) each. I think that probably the easiest way to do it is to roll it out thinly, cut out two rectangles and then re-roll the rest and cut out two further rectangles.

Gently, using a spatula remove the first two rectangles to the baking sheet, place two rashers of bacon lengthwise on each and cover them with the remaining rectangles. Put it in the oven and bake it for about 15 minutes or until they start to change colour. Remove from the oven and leave to cool for a few minutes, then with a very sharp knife carefully cut each rectangle across into six and then make one long cut lengthwise down the middle. Serve them while they are still warm or put them on a rack to cool and reheat them.

# Notes